THE
EMOTIONS
OF
GOD'S
PEOPLE

BOOKS BY MILLARD J. SALL

The Emotions of God's People
Faith, Psychology, and Christian Maturity

MILLARD J. SALL

THE EMOTIONS OF GOD'S PEOPLE

HELPING THOSE WHO ARE HURTING

ZONDERVAN
PUBLISHING HOUSE

OF THE ZONDERVAN CORPORATION
GRAND RAPIDS, MICHIGAN 49506

THE EMOTIONS OF GOD'S PEOPLE

© 1978 by Millard J. Sall

Library of Congress Cataloging in Publication Data
Sall, Millard J
    The emotions of God's people.

    1. Bible—Psychology.   2. Christianity—Psychology.   3. Psychology, Reli-
gious.   4. Psychology—Popular works.   5. Christian life—1960—   I. Title.
BS645.S24   155.2   78-15717
ISBN 0-310-32441-6

Printed in the United States of America

To my oldest sons,
Mark and Tim,
who are following me
into the field of clinical psychology.
I am proud of them for this reason,
but even more so because of
their faith in Christ
and the quality of their personal lives.

Contents

Acknowledgments

I wish to thank the following people: Linda Davies, who typed and then patiently re-typed the manuscript; Myrna Hall, who read the manuscript and gave valuable feedback; and the Reverend Wallace Norling and Pastor Mike Fisher, who contributed helpful comments and criticisms. Thanks most of all to Alan Basham, my editorial assistant and fellow counselor, who took off more than a few rough edges in the style and structure of these pages. His psychological insight and literary skills were invaluable in the process of transforming my thoughts, lectures, and paragraphs into a completed work.

Introduction

Everyone has emotions. Our feelings are our response to what happens to us. God created man with the ability to feel, and so this capacity is good. However, understanding emotions is not an easy task; feelings can be confusing. All of us respond to life in many different ways. We feel joy and sorrow; anger and tenderness; courage and fear; love and loneliness. These feelings, and the way we demonstrate them, reveal the type of person we are.

Emotions, then, are an important part of personality. In fact, as we study personality we come to understand our emotions better. In studying personality, we discover what our emotions are saying and where they come from. For this reason, each study in this book begins by analyzing a type of personality.

Few things create more interest than such a study of human nature. Why do people do the things they do? Why do they react so differently? Why do they choose different occupations? A certain vocation may appeal to one person, while another rejects it without a second thought. People are fascinating, to say the least.

I know a woman whose chief entertainment was to sit in a parked car on a busy street and watch people walk by. She said the expressions on their faces, the way they talked, and the things they looked at in the shop windows were a source of never-ending fascination to her.

Most people will admit that it is our relationships with people that bring our greatest joys in life. They also bring our biggest disappointments and deepest frustration. I believe that the most rewarding experience in life is sharing and working with people: big or little people; angry or happy people; sick people; and, thank the Lord, well-adjusted people. The greatest challenge by far is to understand human nature.

It is the purpose and prayer behind this book that we Christians may have our emotional and spiritual horizons broadened and our understanding of human personality deepened, so that we may be better equipped to cope with the people we encounter day by day. May we gain a deeper perspective on life's perplexing problems and a greater understanding of some of the solutions. May we come to understand that problems are not only rooted in the spiritual dimension; personal problems are complex and multifaceted, and God can use different means to solve them.

Some people believe that God is being left out unless one gives a spiritual answer to every problem of human nature. We need to come to terms with the fact that God is ultimately behind every treatment in which people are helped. All good comes from God, and He wants us to be open to the many and mysterious ways He answers our needs. For example, God guides the surgeon's hand. If a tumor must be removed, the doctor is the one who performs the surgery. But God gave the surgeon his hands and the wisdom to use them; He opened the door for his training; and He provided the instruments that made surgery a success. All good comes from God, and He is in control.

As a springboard for this study of human emotions and personality problems, we will be examining a variety of Bible characters. The information we can gather from them will be used as a foundation for understanding the people we meet in our own lives. People around us each day reveal some of the same problems and personality traits found in Bible characters. We can learn to deal with the psychological nature of those around us, their strengths and weaknesses, much as it is done in the counseling chamber.

It is not my intention to make an inflexible interpretation of the Bible characters, for we can never fully analyze a person we have not met. However, the problems of biblical characters match the problems encountered every day by both Christian and secular psychologists. It might be helpful for the reader to examine my first book, *Faith, Psychology and Christian Maturity*, as background for this study. It will explain basic terminology and help the reader to integrate Christian faith and psychology.

After the Biblical and psychological portraits are complete, practical suggestions will be given so that the reader can help those who are in need of understanding. Merely describing and diagnosing symptoms without helping the reader to help others would be inexcusable. Since we professional counselors can see so few of the people who are troubled, it is my prayer that educated laymen will become involved in helping all people, especially those who suffer with perplexing emotional problems.

Of course, all living situations, illustrations, and names in this volume have been changed to maintain confidence; any similarity to known persons is purely coincidental.

THE
EMOTIONS
OF
GOD'S
PEOPLE

1

What Is
Personality?

Just about everyone knows a girl like Alice. She is attractive, expressive, and entertaining. We say that Alice has lots of "personality." Then there is Bill. He is flat, uninteresting, even boring at times. We say that Bill has no personality.

These descriptions reveal only a small part of the individual's personality type; they are not personality in themselves. The term *personality* refers to more than individual traits blending together to create the mysterious quality that makes one appealing and sometimes even famous. Most people have not thought very seriously about personality; so much of the information in this book may come as a surprise. Let's wade through some slightly technical material that will serve as background for our study of Bible characters.

MASKS AND HOUSES

Each person not only *has* a personality—he (or she) *is* a personality. Personality is his particular style of feeling, thinking, and acting. It includes his behavior in the varied situations of life, his system of interaction with other people, and his feelings about himself. Personality also includes a person's appearance as well as his preferences and inclinations. These aspects of personality help us to cope with internal tensions and to interact with people in daily living.

The psychologist and the professional counselor use the word *personality* to refer to a personal mask like those worn by actors in ancient Rome. This is not to say that we are all fakes; the analogy of the mask points out that although personality is uniquely our own, yet it is on display for all to see. It is not something we put on; it is what we are in relationship to God and each other. Therefore, personality is the combination of all of the behaviors and the defenses each person uses in relating to the world.

We could say that each one of us lives in a mental, emotional, and behavioral house, and each house is unique. For example, a woman may become interested in nursing because as a child she felt that no one was interested in caring for her. As a nurse, she identifies with the patient and thus expresses her deep inner need for love and attention.

Similarly, a man may choose to live alone in the back country of Colorado because he was deeply hurt in a close interpersonal relationship earlier in life. His love of the country seems to act as a balm that repairs his damaged ego. It also serves as a retreat from people who have the potential to hurt him again.

A crooner may be singing of love because it is his greatest need. Everything he does or says revolves around his need to be loved. Another person may have a need to be seen because his family members paid no attention to him as a child. He said, "Dad, watch me jump!" But dad never watched. Or he said, "Mommy, I hurt my ankle!" But mother paid no attention. Now he is driven by an enormous need to perform in public.

Most psychologists agree with a definition of personality that pictures it as a system for relating to the environment as well as being a defense against it. The unique qualities of each "house" reveal the deep needs of the person who lives within. Disagreements over definitions of personality center on the internal causes, or dynamic forces, that produce the various personalities.

Carl Jung, a famous psychologist, believed that we inherit our personality from our ancestors. Some maintain that personality is developed early in childhood and purely in reaction to the world around us. Others hold that it is strictly a question of "genetic predisposition"; that is, people are born with differing sensitivities, so they react differently to the people in their lives. Still others believe that personality is molded solely by spiritual virtues or the absence of them. This view overemphasizes man's sinfulness and concludes that an emotional problem always indicates sin in a person's life. According to this view, the only solution to immature personality traits is conversion. When the person comes into a relationship with Christ, he becomes mature.

The closer we get to the truth, however, the more we discover that the real answer is a combination of these views. We may be sure of one thing: by studying personality we begin to know the facts about an individual, and only then can we come to a fair evaluation of his emotions and character. It is important for us to have a thorough understanding of his life history and to see his present circumstances from a physical, spiritual, and psychological point of view.

SOME HELPFUL TERMS

A study of personality often includes such popular terms as "multiple personality" and "split personality." These terms may be confusing to the layman. Multiple personality means that multiple sets of personality traits exist in the same person, and he manifests them alternatively. That is, he may be a kind, loving person when one personality is functioning, and a bitter, cruel person when an alternate personality predominates. Often the multiple personality is confused with the split personality. The split personality is an individual who has removed himself, split off, from contact with the world around him. He is withdrawn emotionally from people.

QUESTIONS

You may be wondering at this point, "Is *character* different, or distinct, from *personality?*" The answer is basically no. Character, as it is thought of today, is more or less synonymous with personality. However, people do tend to think of personality as the traits they observe, while character refers to the deeper structures of human personality. The term *character*, then, refers to the organization and structure of the personality. It includes the way a person reacts to people and situations and the defenses that help the person cope with anxiety. From this point of view, we speak of "character formation" and "character structure."

Many questions can be asked about a person's character. Some of them are more general. For example: What are his strengths and weaknesses? How does he satisfy his desires and needs? How does he perceive reality? What is his life style and what caused him to choose it?

Other questions are more specific. Why did he go into that line of work? Is emotional impact in his interpersonal relationships high or low? What's going on inside of him? What behavior is distinctive to him? What might we learn if we gave him a battery of psychological tests?

There are also questions that relate to faith and life. Is sin the sole cause of his problem? Can a true Christian have an emotional problem or is it always a case of backsliding? What part would conversion play in this person's life?

We will be seeking answers to questions such as these in our study of personality.

One of the things I have found perplexing in working with Christians is that they are often afraid to understand themselves. As we together uncover deeper motives and drives, they are often shocked to learn that their problem is not purely a spiritual one. It is exciting when these people gain insight into themselves and discover that psychological factors are involved. For example, a person who relates better to ideas than to people may have felt led into the field of mathematics or bookkeeping. A person given to emotional outbursts might choose to be an actor or actress. In each case, the symptoms fit their choice of occupation. Uncovering this truth often frightens Christians needlessly.

It has been my experience that the more we understand our motives and free ourselves of weak or bad motivation, the more we are able to succeed and find fulfillment in our occupations. Discovering the psychological reasons for our choice of occupation does not take away from the concept of a spiritual calling. God uses all of our experiences, the good and the bad in our life, as instruments to place us where He wants us to serve. This does not explain away God's call.

Paul said in Philippians 1:15, 17; "Some, to be sure, are preaching Christ even from envy and strife, but some also from good will; . . . the former proclaim Christ out of selfish ambition. . . ." Paul is saying, in part, that despite the defenses and poor motives of his rivals, he was happy that the gospel was being preached. God uses people—with their hang-ups—and for this we may be ever grateful.

THE PERFECT PERSONALITY

The Gospels concentrate on Jesus' earthly ministry, which extended over approximately three and one-half years, and as a result, much of his life remains obscure. Nevertheless, the Gospel accounts portray Him as a Person of complete emotional maturity. Jesus was also physically healthy; and He was spiritually whole, willingly following the Father's guidance and happy to do His will. Because He is our only Savior, He must have been perfectly adjusted to His environment.

Jesus' ministry shows us that He was people oriented. For example, when He was cornered by opposition, did He withdraw? No, He gave wise, insightful answers to those who challenged Him. He also had the capacity for genuine tenderness; He had feelings. When Lazarus died, Jesus wept openly. Did He bow weakly to the selfish immaturity of others? Hardly! When men were making the temple a merchandise mart, He scattered these hypocrites with a bold flurry of justifiable, controlled anger.

Although the church often pictures Christ as a jellyfish, a holy weakling, He was anything but that. He was fully human, and one of the most mature things about Him was His complete integration of the emotions that give life meaning. He said, "I came that they might have life, and might have it abundantly" (John 10:10).

Jesus possessed perfect character; He perfectly expressed feelings as diverse as tenderness and anger, and as our Savior He was perfectly related to the Father but also fully in touch with people. His life shows us that spiritual and emotional maturity we can achieve through His example and power. He is indeed the perfect personality.

OUR PURPOSE

In the next chapter we will begin a study of various persons in the Bible. Our purpose in each study is to develop a clearer perspective about personality and emotions. We will see the complex factors that influence the development of positive or negative traits, and hopefully we will understand what can be done to strengthen personality weakness. Each study is built on the presupposition that God loves imperfect people. Our purpose, then, is—

1. to enhance your insight into your own character;
2. to help you to become a more fulfilled Christian;

3. to add to your understanding of other people;

4. to increase your motivation to serve the Lord.

The Bible is filled with different types of personalities. Although most biographies tend to play down the bad and accentuate the good, the Bible pulls no punches in telling about people. Whether the person was a sinner or a saint, Scripture tells the story honestly. It presents people in total perspective, rather than whitewashing their lives. The reason for this is given in 1 Corinthians 10:11: "Now all these things happened to them as an example, and they were written for our instruction, upon whom the ends of the ages have come."

Looking at several people in the Bible will help us to understand the emotions of the people you and I meet every day. It is my deepest hope that this book will help your path of life shine more and more until that "perfect day." May you glorify God through the radiance of your personality.

2

Esau,
the Impulsive Rebel

Esau had a problem. Perhaps it is better to say that his life was an unsolved problem in self-control. His downfall was his inability to say no to himself. Unable to control his desires and impulsive behavior, Esau lived for *today*. He ended up a failure and a social outcast, typical of the personality known as a *character defect* or *character disorder*.

Esau's story begins in Genesis 15:24, while still in his mother's body:

> When her days to be delivered were fulfilled, behold, there were twins in her womb. Now the first came forth red, all over like a hairy garment; and they named him Esau. And afterward his brother came forth with his hand holding on to Esau's heel, so his name was called Jacob; and Isaac was sixty years old when she gave birth to them. When the boys grew up, Esau became a skillful hunter, a man of the field; but Jacob was a peaceful man, living in tents. Now Isaac loved Esau, because he had a taste for game; but Rebekah loved Jacob. And when

> Jacob had cooked stew, Esau came in from the field and he was famished; and Esau said to Jacob, "Please let me have a swallow of that red stuff there, for I am famished." Therefore his name was called Edom. But Jacob said, "First sell me your birthright." And Esau said, "Behold, I am about to die; so of what use then is the birthright to me?" And Jacob said, "First swear to me"; so he swore to him, and sold his birthright to Jacob. Then Jacob gave Esau bread and lentil stew; and he ate and drank, and rose and went on his way. Thus Esau despised his birthright. —Genesis 15:24-34

Close examination of his life style and family background helps us see him as a type of personality that exists in our culture also.

The first thing that stands out about Esau is his ability as a skillful hunter, "a man of the field." What are some qualities he would need to be a successful hunter? A good intellect to understand and predict the ways of wildlife; the sly nature of a manipulator, to entice animals into his traps; energy and enthusiasm, to pursue an active career. At first Esau's sly, manipulative nature may seem totally undesirable. However, he was able to make good use of this trait, as well as his intelligence and other gifts, in his occupation. He was unquestionably a great hunter because he was well known for his prowess.

Esau was also a restless, highly active person; and this, too, correlates with his occupation. He is described as a young man who enjoyed the taxing, adventurous life of the chase. He typifies the person who engages in restless activity. When anxiety and tension built up within him he "acted out" by working off his energy and drives.

A Troubled Childhood

In verse 28 we see other things about Esau's personality, things from his childhood that caused him to act as he did. Healthy child development requires an equal amount of love, discipline, and affection from both mom and dad, but in Esau's life the family lines were polarized—split down the middle. Isaac loved Esau because he liked the venison his son put on the table; Rebekah favored Jacob. What was the result of this problem parenting? As we shall see this influenced Esau's development. He became a man who was geared for immediate gratification of his impulses and who was unable to cope with his drives.

The Genesis account of Esau's life and troubles reveals at least three parental influences on his behavior. First, it is most likely that Rebekah's blatant and calculated preference of Jacob constituted a rejection of Esau in his early, formative years. We know that a young child is geared for instant gratification of both his physical needs and his need for love.

When does your little three-year-old want her candy? You may have caramels in the kitchen; there may be chocolates and peppermint sticks in the closet; she may even have a drawer full of Halloween candy stashed away for hard times. Yet, when you and that tiger get to the local supermarket and she discovers the candy counter, how far away does that candy at home seem to her?

The only thing that is real to a young child is the present moment, and that is normal for children. We don't expect them to deal with long-range planning or with abstract thinking. Many adults, however, have never grown beyond this need for instant gratification, the "I want it *now*" syndrome. Like Esau, those who do not receive enough spontaneous love as a child continue their irresponsible search for love or gratification in adulthood.

A baby equates love with gratification, especially in the areas of hunger, pain, bodily warmth, and the comfort of being held. The newborn infant cries *immediately* when he or she wants or needs something. Can you imagine a baby thinking, *Well, maybe it's not convenient for Mom if I cry right now. She'll be in with the bottle pretty soon, and I can wait. Meanwhile, I'll just lie here, play with my toes, and love the world.* Not on your life! He wants that bottle, or he wants to be held, and he wants it *now*.

It is quite possible that Esau was rejected by his mother in his early years. His needs for love and immediate gratification were not satisfied as an infant. Like all children, he would have been tremendously sensitive to this rejection. We may therefore justly reason that as an adult Esau had a need for immediate gratification and love, with little or no tolerance for delay.

The second parental influence on Esau's adult behavior also came from his mother: he identified with Rebekah's cunning manipulation of others. She not only rejected him; she also passed on to Esau aspects of her crafty and manipulative personality. In Genesis we see her plotting to deceive Isaac into blessing Jacob instead of Esau. Isaac had said to Esau, "Prepare a savory dish for me such as I love, and bring it to me that I may eat, so that my soul may bless you before I die" (Gen. 27:4). Hearing this, Rebekah went into action to see that *her* favorite son received Isaac's blessing (Gen. 27:5-14).

She made savory meat to suit Isaac's taste. She put Esau's clothing on Jacob and covered his smooth arms with animal skins so that they would resemble his brother's hairy arms. Rebekah then instructed Jacob to deceive his father, even to the point of lying about a matter considered sacred in their culture—the birthright. She wanted Jacob to receive Isaac's blessing so that he might gain the birthright.

Although Jacob was definitely her favorite and later demonstrated craftiness, Esau, as well, learned to copy mom. By means of his mother's example, he developed the nature of a sly, cunning hunter.

And what of Isaac's influence on Esau? With some careful thought, we perceive that the father had his share of imperfections as well, and that Esau also picked up some of these character traits. When we see the reason given in Scripture for Isaac's preference of Esau, the cat comes out of the bag.

Why did Isaac favor his older son? Was it because Esau was a man of solid character? Was he a great help around the house? Did father and son have many things they enjoyed doing together? No, Isaac loved Esau because of the meat he put on the table. When a man rejects one son and loves the other because of something as trivial as food, we have to accept the fact of an immature motive in the parent.

WORDS DON'T ALWAYS WORK

The influence of Isaac and Rebekah on the character of Esau is an excellent example of a psychological principle known as *modeling*. This principle can help us to understand a problem in many Christian homes.

We can teach and discipline our children continually and strive to share our faith with them, but our words are not enough. It is unavoidably true that children will pick up our bad habits. As one young person said to his parents: "Don't bother talking to me about right and wrong. Your actions are screaming so loud, I can't hear your words." This is why it is so important for parents to be Christ-like in their love for their children and not merely Christian in their values.

Isaac and Rebekah were both people of faith; Isaac is mentioned in Hebrews 11, the well-known chapter that lists stalwart men and women of faith. How is it that the faith of Esau's parents did not become a binding force in his life, though some of their bad traits certainly were passed along? This is also a common problem among Christians today.

You may know parents who reared their child in the church, taught him right and wrong, and attempted to impart a saving faith to him. Yet, when the child is older, he rejects it all and lives a life that breaks his parents' hearts. I have had many distraught mothers call me to say: "I can't understand it. My child was reared in a Christian home, but he is no longer interested." The parents are left bewildered and crushed.

We need to remember that in the earliest years of life, a child has not developed the ability to reason. He cannot look within at his feelings and motives or think rationally about his behavior. Young children make choices and decisions long before they know right from wrong. They develop ego (the relating, decision-making part of personality) long before they develop a conscience. This infant ego is the beginning of a separate identity, but it does not know right from wrong.

As the ego slowly begins to mature, the conscience begins to emerge; the child begins to introspect and look into things. He begins to consider his choices and decisions a bit more deeply. At this stage the development of independence begins. Further, if a child has known only rejection, he will eventually reject his parents' values. The love needs of the infant ego must be met before the conscience will develop sufficiently to be receptive of parental values and life style.

ABOUT CONSCIENCE

Esau might have identified with his parents' positive values, but he was deprived of the love and controls he needed from them. He unwittingly copied the weakness of Isaac and the sly, cunning nature of Rebekah through modeling, while refusing to accept their personal value of a life of faith. Rejected in the early years of his life, he remained a child emotionally.

You may know some chronologically old people who are very immature. They respond differently than would most of society because their emotional growth has been minimal. This type of person never seems to profit from anyone else's experience. In fact, if he has a characterological problem, or what is known as a character defect, it may be possible for him to go through life never able to "incorporate"; that is, he has difficulty taking on others' values or character. He is not able to develop what is commonly called conscience.

You may think of conscience as a little voice inside that

talks to you, mostly saying No!, but it is more than that. Conscience is the internalization within the human psyche of the external command of the parent. Let's see how it works.

After Johnny is told for the third time, "Don't take your milk into the living room" and has his hand slapped for disobedience, he begins to develop a conscience. Johnny will later, in his mind, slap his own hand and voluntarily run back into the kitchen while saying to himself, "No, Johnny, don't take your milk into the living room." He has taken in the parent's command, and it is now living inside of him.

One's parents may be dead for years, but where are all their values, their rights and wrongs? They are still living inside of us, their children. In this sense, our parents are still alive.

The internalization of parents can be further illustrated from dreams. I see my dad in a dream about every three to six months; dad and I are in Colorado where I grew up. We have days at the old swimming hole or rides to downtown Denver. At times we talk in his Colorado Springs apartment, and I can feel his warmth and laughter, though he has been dead since 1958. If I live to be seventy-five, I will always experience him inside of me.

This is not magical, eerie, or supernatural. It happens to anyone who has internalized a thing (such as a value) or a person. If a child has a difficult time incorporating his parents, he will not have the internal reinforcement of his parents' values to guide his behavior. The result is often incredible rebellion against authority or the wishes of any parental figure.

Consider the campus violence of the 1960s. It was more than a desire for new programs, justice and equality, or the ending of a war. The protest movement often escalated to nothing less than a widespread breakdown of obedience to law and respect for authority, *any* authority. This is also why some people hate the church; it is an authority figure. They hate parents. They hate police. They are saying, "If this is what the establishment wants, then it's wrong and I don't want it!"

The detrimental effect of Esau's home environment, then, created an inability to cope with authority and a strong desire to act out hostility in a life style different from his parents. One must have ego needs met and incorporate parental values and commands in order to develop a conscience. Esau was rejected and manipulated, and therefore he developed a defective conscience with poor impulse control. For this reason, although they had a strong faith in God, his parents left little or no mark on their older son. We shall see in the next section how deeply this affected his life.

GETTING NOWHERE FAST!

A closer look at Esau's behavior reveals the results of his character defect. First, Esau could not cope with personal drives; he had no ability to delay his desires. He was a worldly person living outside the sphere of moral sanctity. Hebrews 12:16 refers to Esau as an immoral, godless person. His impulsive acting out of desires revealed a lack of moral character and a tendency toward immorality.

In Genesis 25:30,32, Esau pleads with Jacob for a bowl of stew, claiming to be famished and about to die. His hunger was predominant at the moment, but it is hard to believe that he was at the point of death. Esau was a strong man and a skillful hunter; he would be the last person to starve in the field. Nevertheless, he was hungry enough when he came in from the hunt to lie; he exaggerated his need. He could not deal with his emotions in an adult manner, even concerning his hunger.

Esau also acted spontaneously for immediate gratification. Like Esau, persons with a character defect do not think things through. I had a client like this. As he was walking by a tattoo shop one day, he decided he needed a tattoo. He did not stop to think about why he wanted it, nor did he think more about it afterward. There was the tattoo shop; he had never had one; and he had enough money in his pocket. So he got the tattoo, without ever stopping to think that it is imbedded in the skin and remains visible for life unless it is surgically removed. And even then it leaves a scar.

The person with the impulsive character defect is also easily influenced by others. He is not only impulsive, he is also highly suggestible. For example a young girl from a nice, middle-class home needs to feel loved by her peers; she needs to be "in." A fellow says, "Hey, I have a bit of heroin here; you really haven't lived until you've tried it. You'll feel sexually gratified and free of anxiety right away! Your mind will really fly!" Being a suggestible person, she takes the drug and believes her troubles will melt away.

Can you see the suggestibility in Esau? Here is a cunning man, a successful hunter. Yet he is toppled when his brother says, "Sell me your birthright." The reason for Esau's suggestibility is twofold.

First, he needed love and closeness, which he never received as a child. He does not feel good about himself, so he will do almost anything to gain love and approval. Secondly, because of his lack of maturity he has not developed the ability to objectify. *Objectify* means to consider the facts and project the consequences of our behavior apart from emotional and self-centered thinking. The person who cannot objectify is easy prey for anyone who pays attention to him. Suggestible, impulsive Esau flippantly said to himself, *Well, I don't know why I need that birthright. What good is it to me if I'm going to die of hunger? I'm not going to worry about the future while I'm famished.*

Pressures and frustrations produce strength and stability in an emotionally healthy person. Past experience and emotional growth give us the ability to integrate impulses and drives and make them work for us, rather than destroy us. We learn to think about our desires and impulses, to balance them with responsible behavior. Esau, however, demanded immediate gratification and would not be put off.

To make matters worse, Esau demonstrated an attitude of rebellion against authority. "And when Esau was forty years old he married Judith the daughter of Beeri the Hittite, and Basemath the daughter of Elon the Hittite; and they brought grief to Isaac and Rebekah" (Gen. 26:34-35). Esau hurt his parents deeply by marrying two heathen women.

I frequently receive calls from parents who are grief-stricken at the behavior of their children. Some teens turn to drinking or other drugs simply because it is a way of defying the standards and authority of their parents. I know of at least one teen-age girl who deliberately became pregnant to get even with her parents; she knew it would hurt and embarrass them.

Rebellion is not limited to young people. Adults often drive too fast or recklessly, not because they are in a hurry, but as a way of rebelling against the rules. Tax cheaters defy the law. Wives and husbands hurt each other and strain the marital contract. It is not easy to understand why people do such things, but this behavior may be caused by feelings of poor self-worth and a need to establish omnipotence by overt rebellion or by storing up anger.

The last thing Isaac and Rebekah wanted was for their son to marry a pagan wife, but Esau chose two of them. Scripture tells us that the Hittites were enemies of the children of Israel; so Esau married women who were enemies of his family. His impulsive action must have been heartbreaking to his parents.

A CHAIN OF MISTAKES

When Esau sold his birthright, he made a terrible mistake. He said, in effect, "I will sell my entire inheritance down the drain. I will give it up simply because I am hungry and cannot wait to eat. I want my stew, and I want it now."

What was the importance of the birthright? In early Old Testament times the eldest son in each family was considered to be the family priest. Christ is our High Priest today, the intercessor between man and God. Prior to Christ's first coming, man needed a God-appointed intercessor and God chose Aaron as the first of these. Before the time of Aaron, however, the eldest son and new head of the family received the priestly rights as part of the birthright. The eldest son was honored heir to the Abrahamic promise, and this was no small honor. Esau relinquished this honor for a bowl of stew and therefore lost the blessing that was rightfully his.

In attempting to cover a mistake, the impulsive person will often compound his error. Esau had an immediate need; he wanted to be restored to the good graces of his father. "Now Esau saw that Isaac had blessed Jacob and sent him away to Paddan-aram, to take to himself a wife from there, and that when he blessed him he charged him saying, 'You shall not take a wife from the daughters of Canaan'" (Gen. 28:6).

Esau then made another mistake in an effort to cover his previous failure. He impulsively married another pagan woman. This time it was a Canaanite, another enemy of his family. Perhaps he did this to please his father or to express anger, or both. He may have done this to get even, while at the same time hoping that it would somehow make everything better. He said something like the following: "If dad doesn't like the fact that I married two pagan women and if he wanted me to marry a good woman—one that would please him—then I will marry again." Although it is hard for us to understand, the person with a character defect often does illogical things in his efforts to correct his mistakes. These actions compound the problem he sets out to solve.

Attorneys often ask me why their clients say one thing and then do the opposite. They ask, "Why do they ask me to defend them and then go on to defeat their own case by changing their story?" Such a person is experiencing the manipulation employed by the person with a character disorder. We ask, How can the impulsive person lie with such a straight face? It is because satisfying this need is the only thing that is important to them at the time.

I would be an easy mark for a lie detector. If I were lying, the indicator would probably go off the scale because I can't hide a lie. However, people like Esau would not be good subjects because they really believe they are telling the truth.

Suppose such a person owed you a thousand dollars. His immediate need is to have you like him, so he will promise to have the money in the mail by morning. He may be unemployed and nearly bankrupt, but he ignores the facts. He actually believes that, like magic, he will have your check in the mail by morning. His immediate need is for your approval, so he says what he knows you want to hear.

Similarly, Esau married a third wife to please his father. He decided to get married again, but in anger he married the wrong person. Hoping to solve the conflict magically, he only caused himself a greater problem.

A common example of this chain of mistakes is the married man (or woman) who carries on extramarital affairs. Their immediate need is to receive some gratification that is missing in the home, such as sexual fulfillment or support from their spouse. Rather than face the problem at home and solve it wisely, they parade from one friend to the next, hoping to meet their needs. When the friend begins to depend on them, however, they go to the next person and then to the next, never realizing that the source of their unhappiness is within themself, not in the opposite sex.

This social and sexual labyrinth is like the cotton mill where everything went wrong one day. A new employee failed to get the thread started correctly. As a result, the thread darted here and there and became hopelessly entangled in looms, spools, cutters, dye tanks, the water cooler, and the secretary's new typewriter. The only way to solve the mess was to get to the source and begin untangling. The source in the example above is the person's lack of ego strength and their insufficient development of conscience. If he does not grow to emotional maturity, his attempts to solve his problem will be ineffective.

SHALLOW REPENTANCE

Although he rejected it earlier, Esau wanted his birthright later, when it seemed important. In Genesis 27:34 we find him pleading for his father's blessing, though he had scorned it not long before. In Hebrews 12:17, we read of Esau, "For you know that even afterwards, when he desired to inherit the blessing, he was rejected, for he found no place for repentance, though he sought for it with tears." He sought forgiveness with tears, but did Esau have genuine repentance in his heart?

The word "repentance" in Scripture means "a change of mind," that is, a change of plan or action. This term is even used in reference to God in Genesis 6:6. This means that the Lord changed His mind; He changed His method of dealing with people. Had Esau truly repented, his behavior would have changed. If a person says, "I feel guilty," it does not necessarily mean he regrets his action and recognized his responsibility for it. "I'm sorry" often means "I'm sorry I was caught."

Sometimes convicted criminals show no remorse or guilt for what they have done. Or it may look as if the lawbreaker feels guilty and is sorry when he is brought before the judge. He may even promise never to do it again. But the truth of the matter is that he only regrets being caught.

If Esau had genuinely repented and said, "I goofed and I'll try to change," his actions would have reflected a change of heart. Even his request for his father's blessing would have shown his desire to please God and honor his family. However, Esau was the same person before and after his mistake, so we know that his repentance was not sincere.

Scripture says "the way of the treacherous is hard" (Prov. 13:15) and that "whatever a man sows, this he will also reap" (Gal. 6:7). The Bible passages concerning Esau are a sad commentary on the life of a young man who had both winning characteristics and ability. Esau fades out of view in Scripture after he is listed as a godless and immoral person who lost true happiness and abundant life. He had no depth of character or ego strength to make him a faithful follower of the Lord; his potential was sold for a bowl of stew.

There are many Esau's in our time, and they need to be reached for Jesus Christ. The next chapter will give insight on how to recognize the various degrees of character disorder and how to reach out to help these people change.

3

The Impulsive
Person Today

The effects of impulsive personality problems are all around us. Everywhere we turn we see people behaving in ways similar to Esau. The major symptom of the impulsive personaltity is that he acts on the spur of the moment for immediate gratification. In our society, Esau's problem manifests itself in behavior ranging from simple impulsiveness to cases of severe pathology.

IMPULSIVE ACTIONS

We have all met someone who has a hot temper, who seems to blow off steam first and think about it later. Afterward he says, "Boy, I don't know what got ahold of me. I can't help it; when somebody ticks me off, I just explode." This kind of temper is an example of a lower-level impulsive personality. Such people do not have impulse control; they need to develop the fourth and ninth fruits of the Spirit—long-suffering and self-control.

Another example is the problem of impulse buying. When the lady of the home takes all the children to the grocery store, the bill generally comes out higher. Why? Because children are impulsive and seem to want unnecessary things *now*. Adults have the same problem. You had not planned to buy a new dress or a wood saw, but you did anyway. Although you didn't really need it, the article was appealing and the impulse whispered, "Why don't you buy it?"

The advertising and credit agencies are quite aware of our fallibilities, chief of which may be the tendency to buy things we don't need with money we don't have. Some consumers fight this temptation by making out a list of what they need and buying only these items. This is an effective method for dealing with impulse buying. Woe to the man or woman in our society who has a handful of credit cards but lacks the self-discipline to spend wisely!

The chronic gambler is a more serious impulsive personality; he demonstrates a more serious lack of self-control. Some people live for Las Vegas. Gambling is in their blood, and they have to get there. Regardless of wins or losses, they have to have one last throw at the jackpot. Rarely does an impulsive gambler leave the tables until he is out of money. Later he says, "Why did I blow that money? I'm not going to do something that foolish again." But he does, and the need to gamble intensifies into an emotional disorder.

The alcoholic is an impulsive person with a passive nature. He can do the town or sit at home and get drunk, but in either case he is "sincerely" remorseful the next day.

I remember a particularly enlightening experience with a church member who was an alcoholic. I was a young pastor, and I went over to Harry's the day after his most recent binge. We began to talk about his drinking problem, and he told me, "Oh, what a fool I've been! I've learned my lesson, and I'm never going to do it again." I walked to my car feeling good about the visit. I had really helped him. I had shown him the truth. He had seen the error of his ways and he would not do it again—until the next time the impulse hit him! Superficial confession and remorse do not solve the problem of an immature personality.

The penmanship enthusiast enjoys writing, especially on checks. This enjoyment carries him beyond integrity and common sense to the point where he writes checks without the money to back them up. He did not mean to write a bad check, of course, but it was there in his hand and it was so colorful . . . with a mountain scene, a stream, and a pretty sunset. He thought to himself, *It only takes a minute to fill out a check and it saves you from carrying all that cash. Besides, I don't need to have the money in the bank right now; somehow it will work out all right.* Because of this rationalizing, even people with six-figure incomes can be in trouble up to their neck. No matter how much money they make, they are always in financial difficulty because they cannot control their impulses.

The impulsive liar is another example of the more troubled impulsive personality. The thought process of such a person goes something like this:

> *I'm being interrogated sharply right now, so it's in my best interest to get off the hook. I know what I must say to make you happy. I am being sincere because I really do need to get out of this difficult situation. So I'm not really lying. As long as you hear what you want to hear and the result is in my best interest, then it's the right thing to do.*

By this kind of "magical" thinking, the impulsive liar denies his responsibility, ignores truth and reality, and still believes he is sincere. He is, in fact, the most sincere liar in the world.

Finally, some impulsive personalites such as the sociopath and the schizophrenic manifest clearly psychotic characteristics. Such persons have no impulse control. They do things because their emotions carry them away. They have no conscience about their actions because their ego has not developed sufficiently.

IMPULSIVE PERSONALITY TRAITS

I was once asked why our family keeps chickens and ducks in our back yard. Quite frankly, they add a lighter side to our life. Few animals look as funny as one of our ducks waddling up and down the slopes of the yard. Besides, their singing leaves a great deal to be desired and the chickens always beat them to sunrise and the feeding dish!

As a psychologist I deal with life and death issues nearly every day. In one week I dealt with several potential suicides. That week another of my clients did take an overdose and then attempted to kill herself in an automobile on the freeway. This is serious business, and our ludicrous ducks help to keep balance in my life. We all need to laugh and clown, to be spontaneous, as well as we need to be serious and responsible.

Perhaps by now readers who are excessively concerned with right and wrong, do's and don'ts, shoulds and oughts, are having a field day learning about the impulsive person's inadequacy. It is regrettable that many persons in the church are preoccupied with all that is wrong and are quick to recognize the sins of others. These stoics are some of the most hostile, angry people in the world, and it is no wonder. They are so straight, so locked up with "serious" work that they have no time for childlike fun. They may talk about victorious Christian living, but for them the straight and narrow has become a straightjacket of legalism and narrow-mindedness.

We have touched on the impulsive person's thought processes and impulsive behavior ranging from the hot temper to sociopathic acting out. Many people behave in one or more of these ways, but there are also specific traits that characterize the impulsive personality. These are often more subtle than the behavior listed previously. Once we learn to identify these traits in the person with the impulsive character disorder, we are in a position to help them grow.

The impulsive person deals with the immediate. This trait greatly affects his conduct. This explains why the impulsive personality can act competently so long as the goal is at hand. So he is also a great partygoer because he is so outgoing and expressive. And he tends to have many acquaintances but few lasting friends. Interpersonal relationships are very shallow because he is geared for impulse gratification.

As we observe the impulsive person, it becomes clear that his conduct is governed externally. The only thing that kept Esau from murdering his brother on the spot was the fact that his father was still alive. It is the outside influence that keeps the person with a character defect from doing wrong.

Esau said to himself, *Father is alive, so I can't kill Jacob yet. When dad dies, Jacob has had it!* Note the shallow emotion here. Esau seems to be sorrowing over the approaching death of his aged father, while at the same time plotting to slay his brother.

Chronic impulsive behavior occurs outside of wish, motivation, or decision. For example, a group of youngsters went into a city park where several ducks were swimming in the pond. They cornered one of the ducks and cut off a foot. When asked why they did it, one of them said, "I don't know. We just got the idea, so we did it—we never thought of it before and we didn't think about it later." This cruel act was done on impulse and without any remorse later. If we attempt to discuss such action with the impulsive person, here is how the conversation might go.

"How about that poor duck without a foot? Don't you feel sorry for it?"

"I don't know. I guess so."

"Well, then why did you do it?"

"I don't know. We were just driving around and I kind of got the idea in my head and said to one of the guys, 'Let's do it'; so we did."

Note the absence of any kind of planning; there was no logical thought process involved.

"I didn't want to do it," says another impulsive person, "but I just can't control my impulses." That may be what he says, but his intent is better stated, "I would not do it deliberately, but while I am not looking my hand slips. I can hardly be blamed for that."

I remember a friend with whom I worked in a grocery store. When he brought boxes of chocolates to the shelf, one or two would always get crushed as he went through the door. He would ask, "What can you do with a crushed box of chocolates? We can't sell them and we can't ship them back, so I guess we'll have to eat them. How can I feel guilty about the chocolates when it was an accident? I didn't mean to run into the side of the door; it just happened. How can I be blamed if my hand or foot slips?"

All of this results in a life of discontinuity. Since the impulsive person is only concerned with immediate gratification, the present and future are not related in his mind. This is also reflected in his behavior. Men like Esau suffer from a severe lack of constancy. Their life seems to show little or no realistic progression toward achieving meaningful goals.

When most young men enter a career and start a family they begin to plan ahead and save for retirement. He and his wife buy a home, build equity, save, and invest, hoping to have a comfortable retirement. There is a logical progression to their life that is not found in the person with a character disorder. The impulsive person lives for now.

The impulsive person is selfish. This tendency to live only for today is part of an attitude that says, "The world is mine!" He thinks, acts, and cares only for himself. Relationships with others are superficial and self-seeking. An emotionally mature individual, with a strong ego, can admit he is wrong when he is confronted with a mistake. A strong ego can stand a reversal, but a weak ego cannot. The impulsive person would rather fight and is not willing to give an inch.

Esau became angry with Jacob and blamed his brother for his own mistakes. He wanted his birthright back regardless of his responsibility for losing it. Although he, too, had faults, Jacob was more worthy of the birthright because his faith was more consistent and because he was able to handle responsibility. Esau refused to look at these facts; instead he harbored burning anger for not getting what he wanted when he wanted it. "So Esau bore a grudge against Jacob because of the blessing with which his father had blessed him; and Esau said to himself, 'The days of mourning for my father are near; then I will kill my brother Jacob'" (Gen. 27:41). Rather than admit his mistakes, Esau showed further evidence of his lack of character development by his hatred of Jacob. He even threatened murder and was so convincing in his hatred that Jacob remained wary of him for many years.

His attention is easily captured. Give him an idea, and he will go for it temporarily. He gravitates to whatever strikes his fancy. Bob loves Mary while he is home, but he loves Jennifer when he's out of state. Mary is far away then, so she fades into the background. When he gets home, though, Bob loves Mary again and rationalizes away his unfaithfulness.

For the person with the impulsive character disorder, empathy is possible, but it is defective. He empathizes with the person who helps him to meet his immediate need. He says, in effect, "I will love you if . . ."

At the core, the impulsive problem involves a severe defect in the will. Picture once again the man who says he loves his wife but has now fallen in love with a girl friend. He vacillates between them in a state of confusion and indecision. "I really love them both," he says. "I don't know whether to stay with my wife or divorce her to marry my girl friend." He cannot *will* to do the right thing.

People so often think that love is magical. It supposedly hits you out of the blue, as if falling in love is like falling off a log.

This is a fallacy. Love is a commitment that you work on and develop. It takes a will to love your spouse. If you take your marriage for granted and refuse to work on it, you will soon have problems that will rival the weeds in a lawn during early spring.

What our double-minded Casanova needs to do is to *decide* to remove the girl friend from his life and will to work on his marriage. All the energy he used in coping with two loves could be channeled into loving one woman—his wife. This decision of the will would make for future planning, responsible relating, and a more stable, happy life.

He displays extremely poor judgment. He seems to deliberately avoid accurate planning. His capacity for concentration and reflection is impaired. He rarely answers a question directly. He says things like: "It feels lousy today. I kinda' think I'd like to go to the beach this afternoon." "I don't know. I guess I feel a little hungerish."

With such poor judgment and the inability to think straight, his world becomes one of probabilities. He may begin to write bad checks. He reasons: "I'll probably be able to carry it off without being caught; I'll get the money on credit from somewhere." When he is caught, he admits it did not work out as he planned. He will also usually grant that he knew better.

If you talk about gambling habits to the man who puts too much money on horse races, he will tell you he knows his chances of success are slim and that he did not ask himself the right questions. While he is giving you repentant answers, though, he is planning which horse to play next.

He does not hold himself accountable for his actions. Let's examine some common statements we hear from this person to see how they fit together; this will also help us to see what his thinking is like.

Often he will say, "I just gave in." What is this person saying? This sounds very much like: "I'm a little child. I'm not really accountable for what I'm doing. The world should take

better care of me so that bad things wouldn't happen to me."
Another frequent statement is "I just did it . . . I don't know."
This lack of a sense of responsiblity is due in part to not
thinking through an action.

Imagine that you are at a church banquet, and about halfway
through dinner you spot a twenty-dollar bill lying near the top
of the stairway. You think,

> *I can't just go over and pick it up. What will people think?*
> *. . . But then, someone else might walk by and pick it up. I*
> *could get it and make an announcement, . . . but how will*
> *we know whose it is? Anyone could claim it . . . Since I*
> *saw it first, I should get it. Finders, keepers . . . No, the*
> *money isn't mine . . . I know—we can give it to the church.*
> *Everyone will get the money indirectly, and the problem is*
> *solved.*

Consider the thought patterns that were involved in that
minor decision. Your mind has dealt with guilt, pride, posses-
sion, appearances, fairness, probability, and a workable solution. You thought through what would be the right and wrong
thing to do.

However, the impulsive person might suddenly develop a
terrible cough. To keep from disturbing everyone, of course,
he must go downstairs to the restroom, and on his way he picks
up the money. He feels no pangs of conscience over the fact
that the money belongs to someone else. It never ceases to
amaze me how quickly a twenty-dollar bill can cure a cough!

Other common statements are: "I really didn't mean to do it"
and "I didn't intend to do it." The impulsive person is thinking: *It merely* happened *to me. So I am guilty, but without*
premeditation. If we kill someone, it is better to be convicted of
involuntary manslaughter than premeditated murder. In the
same way, the person with the impulsive character disorder
believes he is only marginally responsible for his actions. So,
he believes he cannot be held accountable for what he does.

He externalizes guilt and responsibility. That is, he blames circumstances or other people for his mistakes. The major assumption behind the rationalizations of the impulsive personality is, "It's really not my fault." He says, "I didn't mean to steal it, but I saw the money lying there on the table and somehow I just took it." He wants you to believe that it is your fault for leaving the money on the table.

I experienced this projection of responsibility firsthand when I sold my '54 Chevrolet for two hundred dollars. The buyer even used my phone to make some long distance phone calls. He didn't bother to pay for either the car or the phone; he explained that he was a good Christian brother and I should trust him to pay eventually. Needless to say, the money never came.

Three months later I went to his home to see about the remaining $185 he owed me. There he was—convicted—I had him! But to my surprise he merely looked at me and said, "You were a fool for selling me the car; you should have gotten the money from me then." I was amazed that this man had no feelings or pangs of conscience about his responsibility in this matter.

The severe sociopath, such as the criminal, uses the following line of reasoning: *Every time I get out of prison, instead of helping me, somebody sticks a gun in my hand*. So you see, if everyone on the outside would quit putting him up to mischief he would not break the law!

He has few enduring values. Few things are sacred for the totally self-oriented man. One such client of mine suddenly became interested in international affairs and particularly the threat of nuclear war. I was pleased that he finally took on a serious matter, until I discovered that this was a get-rich-quick scheme involving fallout shelters. Money was his concern, not human life.

It is amazing how the person with a character defect can use people. In my theological training at Moody Bible Institute, I was assigned to do solo work at a downtown Chicago mission. I learned a great deal in working with the alcoholics and "down and outers" who responded to the call to salvation. Week after week, some of the same men came forward. I am sure that a few were serious, but for most it was purely business. After praying to receive Christ, most of them would ask for a "loan" of a few dollars. So their goal was not repentance and growth; they were manipulating us to achieve a purpose. They thought they would get what *they* wanted—money for alcohol.

He tends to belittle what others consider valuable. This is quite common in our culture. Immature people can be careless or deliberately destructive with others' property, showing little or no concern for what these things mean to the owner. Some people even consider the lives of innocent citizens to be expendable in their drive for power or in their expression of anger.

In this country it is possible to criticize the system and to desecrate the symbols that others hold as signs of their freedom and heritage. Yet these critics often expect to be protected and fed by this system. One of the women in the Manson clan, a group seeking to instill revolution and destroy the American way of life, was collecting welfare. A woman who tried to assasinate former President Gerald R. Ford indicated later that if he had arrived ten minutes later she would not have attempted to shoot him; she would have been picking up her child from school! This rejection of cultural values and the rights of others, while at the same time expecting to be taken care of, is typical of the person suffering from a character disorder.

The impulsive person acts as if the world existed for his pleasure. He even discards friends and beliefs when he has no more use for them. The impulsive man sees a woman as a sex object. The impulsive woman views her husband as a meal ticket or status symbol. Immediate gratification is the only thing that matters; people are disposable.

In this kind of framework, the future holds no meaning or security. The impulsive person does not see that if you work hard as a young man and save, you will be secure in older years. Most people see the future in terms of past experience; the more experience we have in controlling our impulses, the more we are able to act responsibly. Esau's type places no hope in the future; the future cannot be trusted. His present is fragmented and erratic, so the future will be fragmented also. Because of his present instability, he sees only an unstable future.

Ask a young person on drugs about the future, and what will he predict? One told me he expected the government to fall in five or ten years. The future will fall apart, so why plan? It makes no sense to prepare for a future that might never come. This kind of reasoning leads inevitably to the impulsive life style: "Eat, drink, and be merry, for tomorrow you die."

Imagine that you have just received word that you will die in two weeks. You have no family—no parents, wife, husband, or children—and you don't trust in God. You believe that when you die, that's all there is. Would you worry about responsibilities such as your job, your diet, or your savings? Of course not! You might even stop planning and begin living for right now.

In summary, we can say that the actions of the person with the impulsive character disorder are abrupt and without forethought. They lack continuity and are generally unplanned. He has, in a sense, a short circuit in the normal thinking processes. By comparison, let's examine the normal thought processes of an emotionally mature adult.

Right Thinking Is Balanced

We all get a whim now and then: we would like to fly to Hawaii or buy an expensive car or quit our job and go fishing. However, the mature person does not become so totally caught up in the whim that he forgets where he is in life. He experiences the whim without having to act on it. If it is to continue to be entertained in an adult personality, the whim must first become a want or desire and then a sustained desire which requires planning. Old plans are altered realistically, and the new plan is carried out in full awareness of existing priorities. This process is quite efficient. It grants some but not all of our wishes, while maintaining a healthy balance between fantasy and reality.

Here is how the mature thought process works in an everyday situation. We thought of having a waterfall in the backyard of our new home. As a child I had a stream in my backyard in Utah, and there are few things I appreciate more than the sound of running water. So off I went on the idea of building a waterfall. I soon discovered that the lowest estimate for a landscaped waterfall was fifteen hundred dollars. My neighbor told me it had been his experience that a waterfall collects algae and insects, as well as being difficult to clean. My whim had run headlong into reality.

I began to ask myself some questions. "Is it what I really want? Can I afford it? Would the maintenance costs be too high?" Over a period of time, the decision was made *not* to have the only waterfall in the neighborhood. Instead as a family we researched and created a landscaped backyard that gives us a bit of the country feeling we appreciate. Mature thinking may start with a whim, but often undergoes alteration before it becomes a logical and workable conclusion.

Suppose you wanted to be a dentist. You need to examine what a dentist really does. Do you want to stand on your feet most of the day and examine teeth? Do you have good manual dexterity? Do you want to go to school that long? After facing the cost of the education, the time, the expense of setting up a practice, and the function of a dentist, you decide whether or not to be a dentist on the basis of logical thought.

Objective reality is the only thing that stabilizes the whim or impulse. In his egocentricity, the impulsive person does not think in terms of his total life situation. At the moment of his impulse, he thinks only of himself, not the real world. Whims come and go, but a mature person considers such things as cost and the reactions of other people.

When I was a youngster, I took apart an old broken Victrola to see what made it work. As dad and I were putting it back together, the thing that amazed me most was the governor, which was made of weights and springs. When the turntable reached a certain speed, the angle of the governor would change. This kept the speed of the turntable consistent and made for a pleasant sound.

We decided to remove the governor to see what would happen. The sound was terrible—78 rpm records played at twice the normal speed! The phonograph went haywire without its controlling unit. There was no balance. In the same way, the governor that balances life is the ability of the person to relate to people.

How to Help the Impulsive Person

Scripture teaches us to bear each other's burdens, to get involved with people, and to share the things God has given us. Most of us take for granted the level of emotional health with which the Lord has blessed us, but we need to share our maturity with others in a nonjudgmental way. The impulsive person is one who definitely needs our help.

You must understand his problem and how he got that way. There is some basic knowlege that makes it easier to approach the impulsive person. Let's review some of the childhood factors that foster the impulsive character defect.

First, this child usually has either an inconsistent model or no model at all with which to identify. This was the situation in Esau's family. Isaac was inconsistent and pliable, and Rebekah was so involved with Jacob that she had no time to be a mother to Esau. She may have said, "Of course I love you, Esau," as mothers are prone to do. However, her actions did not match her words, and her inconsistency toward Esau was blatant. Isaac, of course, claimed the patriarchal headship of his home, but he, too, was inadequate as a model.

It is easy to see the effects of giving a child much love and affection for the moment, only to take it away abruptly. Mother may go into the hospital for six months, and the child receives little affection. Or consider the little boy whose father is in the Navy. His world revolves around his dad. Six months of the year dad is home giving his son all the love and attention he needs, and the other six months he is out on the high seas. The child gets a lot of love for a while, and then he gets nothing. What does the child learn from this? He thinks: *Get it while you can . . . don't count on the future to take care of you. Be sure you get everything you want and get it now.* The child learns to live for immediate gratification because he has no concept of a stable future.

Another modeling problem occurs when the parents are so strict and demanding that the child finds it impossible to please them. No matter what he does, his parents are not quite satisfied. Their statements of "I love you" are punctuated with "You're bad" so the child never knows where he stands. This harshness causes the child to give up. He learns that it is useless to try to behave, because unless he is perfect he will be punished anyway. He decides, rather, to play the game of getting all the gratification he can between each negative encounter with his parents. He drops out of the growth process altogether.

Occasionally a genetic or childhood illness can contribute to the impulsive disorder. One bright young man I counseled had impulsive traits that resulted at least in part from colic he experienced during the first six months of his life. He had never known when the stomach pain would start or stop, so at a very early age he "learned" that security and feeling peaceful are at best temporary things. Get them now, or you might not get them at all.

The regression or "fixation" (the partial arrest of emotional development) that plagues the impulsive person, then, was quite beyond his control at the outset. A child cannot help reacting to an unstable or harsh environment. If his family moves constantly, he will never develop a sense of permanence and security. If he is given lots of love and suddenly finds it gone, he will learn not to depend on others. He will learn to use them to get what he wants. If his parents are unstable or if they are severely critical, his personality growth will be stunted.

What can one *do* to help the impulsive person?

As you relate to him, strive for consistency. He needs consistent involvement with mature adults. The impulsive person is fearful that you will love him now but not later. He thinks, *You'll get tired of me soon and drop me like a hot potato*. This is the adult version of his childhood frustration, and to make his system come true, he will do things such as tell you off, give you a hard time, or insult you. In short, he will put on every kind of unusual behavior you can imagine, just to give you reason to leave him. This person is testing you to see how much you will take. He is providing you with a reason to leave so that he will not make the mistake of trusting you and then be dropped later.

While most people will walk on lake ice if it is five inches thick, the impulsive person wants to drive a tank, three diesel trucks, and a forty-mule-team wagon over it just to make sure. In response to his immaturity, be as consistently available as possible. Impulsive clients have called me at all hours of the night just to see if I am there. They have a very hard time trusting, so they go to extremes trying to make sure it is safe.

The consistent understanding the impulsive person receives from his friends also helps to counteract the damage done by "hot and cold" parents. One minute dad was upset and demanded instant, ironclad obedience from the kids; next time around, though, he was in a good mood and the children did whatever they wanted. This inconsistent parenting teaches the child to manipulate in order to get what he wants, and it gives rise to the inclination to throw out all restraints on his behavior.

Set firm, loving limits on your impulsive friend. At first he may not like it. However, one client told me after a particularly difficult struggle, "You know, when you set limits I know you really care about me. Mom didn't care whether I got in at ten o'clock or two o'clock. She never even asked. I don't think she cared who I was out with or what I was doing, but I think you do."

Setting limits and expecting responsible behavior are not popular in our society. The trend toward overly permissive parenting has done more than its share of damage. Our fear of damaging the child's personality through constructive discipline has resulted in children becoming totally undisciplined adults. A child raised without limits will feel that he can have whatever he wants and he can have it now, and that is unhealthy.

When the child or the impulsive adult learns that there are limits and standards set by society, he begins to develop internal control over his own impulses. So set limits so that your friend learns how far he can push you. This is one of the most loving things you can do for him.

As we explained earlier, impulsive behavior is a deep problem of the human will, so confront your friend with this problem. He *can* function maturely if he chooses to. The Bible has a great deal to say about the will. "If any man will come after me . . ." (Matt. 16:24 KJV). "Whosoever will let him take the water of life freely" (Rev. 22:17 KJV). The question is, Does the alcoholic really want to stop his immature acting out? Does the unfaithful husband really want his marriage to work? If we reach his will, he may begin to change. The will is decisive.

The impulsive person mistakenly believes that his acting out is good rather than destructive and irresponsible. Rather than deal with problems internally, he lashes out at society or at least acts out his problem. This is his defense against dealing with his inadequacy, and this is the real source of his troubles—himself.

One client had a symbolic way of acting out her impulses. When difficulty arose, she would jump in her car and drive for hours. She was acting out her feelings, but she was also running from her responsibility for her impulses. In the middle of the night she would call me from a phone booth and ask, "What should I do? I'm down here in the middle of Long Beach. I was upset, so I got in the car and drove. I couldn't help myself."

This woman was trying to get away from a situation she did not want to face. By getting in the car and leaving she thought she could make the trouble go away magically.

In a sense, she was also looking for someone or something to solve her problem magically—to give her what she wanted immediately and make everything pleasant again. In counseling, I gradually helped her to understand what she was doing and helped her face her need and the feelings underlying this need. This stopped the acting out, and she began to develop control over the impulses from which she had been running.

When your impulsive friend slips, keep up the dialogue. When he needs to act out his impulses in anger, such as taking off on an aimless drive or drinking excessively, get him to sit down with you and talk it out. Ask questions such as: "What are you feeling? Why do you feel that way? What would you like to do about it?" His answer might be: "I'd like to take every piece of furniture in this room and slam it against the wall." The fact that he is talking about his impulses instead of throwing furniture shows that he is moving away from acting out and he is beginning to organize impulses in his mind.

Try to find out what triggered either the impulse or the episode that results from acting out the impulse. Is he trying to get attention? Is he trying to shock you? Is he testing you again? Is he trying to impose punishment on himself that he thinks he deserved but did not receive? Try to help the impulsive person gain insight into what is behind his actions. He needs to recognize his tendency to manipulate others for his own security. "Why" is the question that leads to understanding his behavior.

Direct the impulsive person toward formation of long-term goals. The impulsive person lives only for now and does not trust the future, so it is good to encourage him to plan ahead. Ask questions such as: "Where would you like to go to college? What would you like to study? What year would it be feasible for you to graduate? What advantages do you see in having a college degree? What will it give you that you don't have now?" This planning for the future causes him to think logically and accurately. Developing long-range goals will alleviate some of the aimless clutter in his life. Instead of erratic, nonsensical behavior, he will advance to a higher level of adjustment. Keep in mind that such a step will not be easy; it goes against the grain of a behavioral system that has been years in the making. Be patient.

The impulsive person must learn to face his responsibility. Often he will skip from friend to friend or from job to job. He might say, "Boy, I don't want to work there any more! The boss is a real jerk—he must be on some kind of an ego trip, telling me what to do." At work, as soon as he encounters structure or some demand is made on him or an inconvenience occurs, this immature person blows up, quits his job, and drifts somewhere else. To combat this, help him face his responsibility.

I believe that a born-again experience with Jesus Christ and the spiritual aspects of a Christian life can be integral in the treatment and correction of character disorders. It is the focal point of the methods used by effective organizations such as Teen Challenge. Many persons who seem to be hopeless cases of drug addiction and irresponsible behavior come to know Christ. Others witness a dramatic change in their behavior.

This is not difficult to understand. What is the impulsive

person doing when he accepts Christ? First, he is identifying with a Person who is consistent, loving, and strong. What does faith in Jesus do for the impulsive person? Our Lord is the same yesterday, today, and forever. The person with a character disorder has never experienced that kind of relationship. He thinks everything is in a state of flux. Therefore, it is most helpful to share Scripture verses with him that point to the solidarity of God. Whether we are rich or poor, sick or well, right or wrong, Jesus never forsakes us.

In identifying with Jesus Christ as Savior, the new Christian has a stable identification. For the first time, there is eternal help. If he can identify with Christ, he has a new self and the possiblity of being a whole person.

An integral part of the Christian life are God's standards of behavior for His children. The Bible says, "He who has My commandments and keeps them, he it is who loves Me" (John 14:21). When one comes to know Christ as Savior, he not only identifies with a person, he also receives a complete set of mature values—the Christian value system. He begins to learn what is right, what is wrong; what is true, what is false. He develops structure in his life. Through identification with Christ, he now has standards that begin to establish some continuity in his life.

4

Obsessive-compulsive:
The Structured Mind

Our study of biblical personalities leads us next to a very common type of individual known as the obsessive-compulsive. These highly structured, hard-working people are solid citizens who contribute a great deal to society in the way of production, management, and research. The obsessive-compulsive person is rational and organized; he gets the job done quickly. His major drawback is the gulf that exists between his emotions and intellect. This personality type is characterized, then, by a need to deal with facts and details in order to keep from feeling deep emotions.

What does the term obsessive-compulsive mean? Obsessive behavior consists of ritualistic thinking. This thinking involves rigidity, a lack of tolerance for the opinions of others, and narrow-mindedness in general. A mild form would be a need for structure and organization—a place for everything and everything in its place. Extreme obsession is typified by the unfortunate person who avoids his feelings by repeating numbers over and over in his head. Compulsive behavior is the acting out of rituals. For example, some people wear only one color or drink only one kind of soft drink. Variety and spontaneity threaten them. Extreme compulsion includes such things as washing one's hands several times after each meal or driving around the block several times before pulling into the driveway. Both obsessive and compulsive behavior are repeated ritualistic defenses; one involves thought and the other involves action. Thus the inclusive term "obsessive-compulsive." Throughout this chapter obsessive-compulsive traits will be referred to as simply "obsessive," for the sake of clarity.

As we look into Scripture, we find the clearest picture of obsessive tendencies when we meet the Pharisees. Matthew 23 describes the rigid, intellectual nature of obsessive behavior. Of course an obsessive person is not necessarily a Pharisee in the classical sense of the hypocritical religionists who coldheartedly put Jesus through a mock trial and had Him crucified.

I am using the Pharisees to illustrate the obsessive personality type because both of them become involved in detail and structure and miss the weightier matters of human involvement. Not all Pharisees were obsessive, to be sure, and certainly not all obsessive person are hypocritical. Yet, the obsessive person today and the Pharisees in Jesus' day show themselves to be active, organized people who believe strongly in what they are doing. Both groups also manifest a tendency to avoid feelings by concentrating on detail, structure, and intellectual exercises.

We should also remember that obsessive traits are no indication of spiritual condition. Obsessive persons may be born-again or unregenerate, as is true with all the personality types discussed in this volume. A man may be truly a child of God and yet possess many traits of the obsessive personality type. A man with a more balanced approach to life and a healthy attitude about himself and others may still be spiritually lost. The Lord does not reach us because of our personalities; He responds to our willing hearts.

DEAD MEN'S BONES

Matthew 23 contains a powerful message from the Lord about the Pharisees and their shortcomings. This chapter reveals false pretenses in their lives.

> Woe to you, scribes and Pharisees, hypocrites, because you devour widows' houses, even while for a pretense you make long prayers; therefore you shall receive greater condemnation (23:14).

Pharisees were dependent on ritual. They were obsessed, as it were, with organization and the appearance of orderliness and structure in their religion. Then, as now, some men prayed in elaborate rituals.

Apparently it was more important to the Pharisees to make a convert than to minister to the real needs of the people around them.

> Woe to you, scribes and Pharisees, hypocrites, because you travel about on sea and land to make one proselyte (23:15).

These obsessive persons were also more concerned with fine detail than with what was happening in the world of people.

> You blind guides, who strain out a gnat and swallow a camel! (23:24).

It takes no great amount of study to see that the Pharisees were overly concerned with details. These religious leaders had added hundreds of minute regulations to the Mosaic law by the time of Christ. They accosted Jesus and His disciples for picking a handful of grain on the sabbath. Their giving to God and man was a show intended to meet social requirements, not a manifestation of thankful feelings. Their religious system bound them to a ritualistic, detailed performance ethic.

> Woe to you, scribes and Pharisees, hypocrites! For you tithe mint and dill and cummin, and have neglected the weightier provisions of the law: justice and mercy and faithfulness; but these are the things you should have done without neglecting the others (23:23).

Pharisees were "blind guides, who say 'Whoever swears by the temple, that is nothing; but whoever swears by the gold of the temple, he is obligated'" (23:16). Obviously, the temple and what it stood for in Jewish culture were more important than the gold in its walls and within its coffers. The Pharisees, though they were highly intelligent, were ignorant of and insensitive to the true meaning of the temple. Their life style was characterized by lack of understanding, a blindness and insensitivity to real values. They were out of touch with their own feelings and those of others.

From other places in Scripture we know that the Pharisees were argumentative. They asked picky questions in order to trap Jesus or to get Him into an argument. They asked:

> Tell us therefore, what do You think? Is it lawful to give a poll-tax to Caesar, or not? (Matt. 22:17).

They also questioned his authority to teach, and they surrounded His disciples while arguing that they should have washed their hands before they ate. They even accused Jesus of being in league with Satan and using the devil's power to perform miracles.

Matthew 23:25 illustrates typical obsessive emotion: "For you clean the outside of the cup and of the dish, but inside they are full of robbery and self-indulgence." Obsessives, like the Pharisees, appear to be extremely kind and pleasant, but inside lies a world of angry, hostile feelings. The expression "killing you with kindness" is tailor-made for the Pharisees. They seem to be wonderful people, but the secrets they lock up inside themselves tell a different story.

The Pharisees, then, lacked a sense of identity; they were polished shells filled with chaos. As Jesus said, "You are like whitewashed tombs which on the outside appear beautiful, but inside they are full of dead men's bones and all uncleanness" (Matt. 23:27). The Pharisees as well as the obsessive person today, were not aware of their emotions. Their rigidity, insensitivity, and preoccupation with structure and detail were all means of denying who they really were and what they were really feeling.

THE DRIVEN PERSON

Several major characteristics typify the obsessive person, and knowing these characteristics helps to identify this personality type.

The obsessive person drives himself incessantly. Everything is tense, deliberate, and full of effort. The catchword of his life is "should." "I should go to church on Sunday." "I should listen to the sermon." "I should be grateful for all the things others have done for me." (Note that he doesn't really *feel* grateful; he thinks he *should* feel this way, so he acts grateful.) "I should be more friendly to that new couple." "I should work on my marriage more." "I should take the kids out." "I should get that extra report done for the boss."

He is, in fact, his own overseer. He gives himself commands, he makes demands on himself, and he even sets deadlines. Then he issues himself directives, reminders, and warnings to keep his performance up.

Even the obsessive person's leisure time is structured. Of all the people in the world, he needs to rest and relax. But he is his own unyielding boss, so he never gets to unwind. He tries, but he cannot seem to enjoy himself and take a break. He even takes great care in planning his leisure time. He thinks:

> *I've been going hard all week, and I'm going to take it easy this weekend. I'll work in the yard from nine to noon, but*

I'll need at least a full hour of complete relaxation from noon to one. I'll just go out to the backyard and lie down and rest. And I'll stay right there for an hour.

Rather than leave his weekend open for whatever he feels like doing, he structures it. The lack of structure frightens him. As a result he never really rests at all. Is it any wonder the obsessive person often drops from a heart attack at an early age?

The obsessive person never "loses himself" in entertainment. Imagine him watching a television program with the overemotional hysteric (chapter 5). The hysteric would be captivated by the show immediately and he would identify with the characters. But the obsessive person would be thinking:

How do they make that crash look so real without hurting anyone? I wonder how they made the background for this scene? . . . This is a new TV and it seems to have a little better color than others I've seen. This looks like a twenty-three—no, a twenty-five inch set. It probably loses a little color from the large screen size. If the set was smaller, the color would be even better.

Notice that he did not become involved in the story. When watching TV, the obsessive person does not get lost in the plot or identify with the characters. He does not cry with the loser or triumph with the winner. He stays lost in his own thought-life—checking out the shape of the plastic molding on the set, the decibel level in the room, and other technical details.

However, even constant thinking cannot keep the obsessive person's feelings totally repressed. The one emotion he may show is anger. An observant person can detect the hostility that lies underneath his controlled, businesslike exterior. These angry feelings may emerge in the heat of debate. Although he will not readily admit to being angry, the obsessive person will often become angry when he is opposed or when it seems he is about to lose control of a situation.

He displays constant and intense concentration. He is like an archer; the harder he pulls back the string, the less the wind will affect the arrow in flight. The more the obsessive person thinks and the harder he concentrates, the less chance there will be for any emotional impact on him. He thinks all the time so that he doesn't have to feel.

The obsessive person has an extreme need to accomplish. He is so completely structured and maintains such an intellectual approach to life that people who allow themselves to experience emotions have a difficult time reaching him. Rather than slowing down and facing his feelings, he becomes activity oriented. He concentrates on producing a tremendous amount of work, and he seeks to accomplish this giant task in a socially acceptable manner. Because he feels constant pressure to perform and to have everything in order, his interpersonal relationships also lack spontaneity. Forced jokes, forced friendliness, forced interest—all this without the light of spontaneity and happiness. His marriage, his career, his social relationships, and even his faith are marked by a rigid, tense level of activity.

His interpersonal relationships are hindered by a pervasive inattentiveness. This person may be talking to you, and yet he seems to be paying no attention to you as a person. We have all heard of the absent-minded professor. This stereotype of intellectual ability in combination with forgetfulness and inattentiveness is really quite accurate. Both the nature and causes of this lack of attention to others point to an intellectual approach to life.

He is preoccupied with facts. The obsessive person is always thinking. This is how he avoids dealing with feelings. "Compulsion"—the strong, usually irresistible impulse to perform an act that is contrary to the will of the subject—sets in when he needs action to reinforce his rigid, defensive thought processes. If he is always busy dealing with facts and details, it is obvious he will have no time to feel or think about others.

He may seem to be talking to you; but he is in fact only relating to the facts he or you is offering. He is not relating to you as a person. He is listening to you to pick up information. This constant collection and sorting of facts creates a very rigid person with a very opinionated nature. This is why the obsessive person can be blind to another person's point of view.

A high-level executive arrived for a counseling session and, as we had done throughout our sessions together, I asked him to lie on the couch. Although much of my counseling is done without the use of a couch, obsessive persons need to relax, to let go of structure and control in order to find their feelings. This man was coming along quite well in our treatment of his obsessiveness. However, this day he did not want to lie down until he told me something.

"I've never been able to look anybody in the eye," he said. "Whenever I'm with someone, I always look to the side or over their head—anywhere to avoid looking at them. I want to see if I can really look you in the eye."

This man had discovered something he wanted to correct, so he had structured a block of time for "solving" the problem. As he marched into my office he was telling himself, *Up till now I haven't been able to look you in the eye, so today I will command myself to look right into your eyes.* His attempt to solve his problem was sincere, but he was dealing only with the facts—where his eyes focused. He was paying attention to where he was looking; he was not paying attention to me. Incidentally, he looked me in the eye for several moments and then went to the couch.

The obsessive personality manifests an inability to relate to others and a tendency to drive himself endlessly, and this is a most unfortunate combination. He is not a free man at all; he is constantly "uptight" and tense. This tension gives us a key. What part of his personality is doing all of this harsh driving?

The obsessive person has a superstrict conscience. Either he had one or two very strict and demanding parents with whom he identified or there was no structure and guidance provided for him in the home. In the latter case, he reacted against the lack of structure and security and set up his own internal system. He became his own harsh, demanding parent. In either case, he has an overactive conscience that demands perfection—the best and more.

THE RESULT: OVERSTRUCTURE

A number of years ago I was invited to debate the head of the philosophy department at a state university on a campus television station. The program was taped and shown later, so my children got to watch their dad on television while he was sitting in the living room with them. That was quite an unusual experience for them, and it took a bit of explaining. At any rate, the professor was an excellent speaker and he knew his field. He discussed the strengths and weaknesses of existentialism and gave an accurate account of the philosophy of rationalism. He knew all about the pessimism of Nietzsche; he could discuss idealism; and he was well-versed on every major world religion.

As I came to the end of our time together, I asked, "Doctor, I wonder where you fit? What do you believe? What are your own philosophical convictions?" But all he did was keep repeating what Socrates, Plato, and others had said. He was in fact admitting that he did not know what he believed or what he really felt. He was an IBM machine loaded with facts about what might be believed, but he did not have the strong personal convictions that flow from the integration of emotions and intellect.

He is given to discussion and argument. A discussion with an obsessive person can be quite frustrating because they concentrate on the facts. Although he will state his case firmly and back it up with facts, you can never be sure he believes what he is saying. It is not that he is lying to you. Rather, obsessive persons generally lack deep conviction. While he is giving you all the facts, you begin to sense that he has no real convictions about the issue. He is discussing for the sake of discussing.

The Pharisees, too, were preoccupied with discussing their religion; they missed the meaning and eternal value of faith in God. In the same way, the obsessive person today is more concerned with the argument and its related facts than with the issue.

I remember two men who were authorities in theology. They would discuss endlessly the fine points of theology, sometimes rising to the heights of fury. They had points and subpoints, proofs and couterproofs for every issue you could think of. As soon as one of them managed to persuade the other, they would jump to another subject and battle again. They were not interested in the issues. I am not even convinced they were concerned with the ultimate truth of God's Word. They were much more concerned with the intellectual battle over facts.

As has been stated in many psychological studies, an obsessive person can be a learning machine. In therapy with the obsessive person, a psychologist might say, "I know that you are telling me about your situation, but how do you feel about it?" The person would respond, "Well . . . I don't know what you mean by that." He will then go right on and give you more details.

In counseling, the obsessive person may be able to remember his childhood in great detail. For example, he remembers his mother shutting him out of the house in the middle of the night, and he was terrified. The neighbors called the police, and an officer named Westlake came over and talked the parents into letting him back into the house. He can remember all the details without expressing any feelings.

He finds it difficult to fit into an unstructured situation. The obsessive person generally misses the tone of social situations, though he may appear to be friendly and outgoing. It is hard for him to cue in on what is happening in social gatherings and to become involved in it spontaneously.

Perhaps you've taken note of such a person after church when everyone is standing around chatting. He walks up to one group, says hello, and then leaves in less than a minute or two. He then stops at another group, greets one or two persons, and then wanders off again. He finds it difficult to engage in light conversation with anyone for ten or fifteen minutes. Unless there is an argument going on or a hot issue to debate, he is lost. He feels nothing; therefore he is quite alone when others are sharing what they feel about the Lord or about other topics.

In a typical group conversation his defenses might cause him to think:

> *She told a joke and four people laughed, so it must be funny. I'd better laugh too because that's appropriate.* Ha! Ha! Ha! *I want it to look like everything is fine and that I'm with it. Got to keep in control of the situation. Don't want to be out of place.*

He relates indirectly to people. Imagine a pilot flying "blind" at night; he is operating his aircraft by means of instruments. He flies as if he were seeing outside the cockpit; but, in fact he is only relating to the outside world through instruments. He may make it to his destination safely, but it certainly will be a colorless flight.

When I am flying I like to see sunshine and clouds, terrain and coastline. I want to experience the flight as well as rely on instruments for control and safety. The obsessive person, on the other hand, spends his whole life flying on instruments. His intellectual approach gets him through in most cases, but he misses the joy of living.

The obsessive deals with people on a purely factual basis. He does not share feelings or deep needs or meaningful conversation with another person. Unless a person matches his formula for living or fits into a project he needs to complete, he finds it difficult or worthless to relate to them. The obsessive relates with people to the extent that they help or hinder his performance system. He sees them as instruments, not as individuals who are valuable in themselves.

He has difficulty making decisions. This is due to his tendency to deal with facts and his overactive conscience. He thinks of five or six reasons to act one way and then counters with reasons to choose the opposite course. As he is weighing minute details, his conscience is telling him, *Don't you dare make a mistake. You have to make a good decision. Do exactly the right thing, so things will go right. Don't let things get out of hand.* His fear of failure and concentration on facts and the opinions of others cause the obsessive person to struggle as he tries to decide what to do. He may appear to be in perfect control of the situation, but he is actually wrestling more with his own demands than with the problem.

Extreme obsessive-compulsive behavior immobilizes a person. The man afflicted with this type of neurosis finds himself thinking the same thing over and over. Imagine what it would be like to have an advertising jingle playing over and over in your head to block out stark terror. Or imagine feeling so guilty about matters of right and wrong that you constantly wash your hands as a symbol of internal purification. Obviously, a person who experiences these kinds of obsessions and compulsions should seek professional help immediately.

THE TREADMILL

The obsessive person lives under more pressure than most of us imagine possible. It seems to be goal-directed pressure, but, in fact it has no direction. The obsessive person is always working, always striving, but his goal is an illusion. His duties are never-ending, so he gains no real peace of mind. His mental and physical activity is geared toward stifling feelings rather than toward accomplishing anything.

This constant physical and mental activity level is like a

man running on a treadmill. He runs hard, expending great amounts of energy, and he has no time for anything that interrupts the running. Nothing surprises him or interrupts him, because he cannot slow down. He is concentrating on the race he has set for himself. He becomes angry at anyone who gets in his way or threatens to slow down his pace. He believes he can run better than anyone else, so he doesn't want your help.

This person spends his life on the treadmill alone. A crowd may gather to cheer his efforts, but no one can join him because he refuses to let anyone get that close. The whole point of his race is to keep others away from him and from his fear that he is a weak person. The race has no meaning, though he does not know it and could never admit it.

The obsessive person can also make unrealistic demands on others. He tends to cast the first stone. Because of his judgmental attitudes, he is quick to throw rocks at someone else's glass house. He is dogmatic and opinionated and cannot tolerate lack of conformity to the status quo, which he defines for himself and others.

The Pharisees were dogmatic and rigid about the fine points of the Law, while ignoring love, which is the heart of the Law. They were quick to judge and reject others, while maintaining a façade of piety. They were not inclined toward mercy or forgiveness. They were quick to use their legalism to throw stones at those who did not practice their system of intellectual religion.

Notice how angry and upset they became when One came on the scene who did not follow their misguided precepts. Jesus spoke the truth, and lived the truth because He was, and is, the Truth. He was in touch with the love and forgiveness of God, not just the omnipotence and righteousness of His character. The Pharisees were quick to oppose Jesus because He was a threat to their controlled religion.

Today's obsessive person is the first to oppose changes of

any sort. Change in the established order is threatening, so he will think of any number or reasons to keep things as they are. He despises those who are spontaneous and free. Because he is not experiencing the joy of being truly alive and free, he condemns those who are. Artists, poets, eccentrics, vagabonds—all are considered inferior, simply because they are different.

Obsessive behavior can also inhibit the church's attempt to reach others for Christ. For many obsessive personalities church is a ritual: doxology, hymn, pastoral prayer, Scripture reading, special music, and then the sermon. If a person is unduly concerned with order and uniformity in worship, he will miss the blessing of communicating with the Lord.

ROLES

The obsessive person relates primarily by means of roles. For instance, as long as he is the doctor who is treating the patient, he gets along fine. If he is an engineer and you have an engineering problem, he will gather others around and solve your problem for you. As long as he can work on an idea or problem, he feels fine. Take away his title—his role—and immediately he feels threatened and insecure.

Imagine a group of church friends on the volleyball court. When an attractive woman walks up to our rigid friend and pats him on the back, he nearly comes unglued! If he had known in advance that she was a spontaneous, affectionate Christian, he could prepare for her expression of appreciation of him. He could even cope with a warm hug because he had planned how he would respond. But catch him off guard and show your feelings about him, and he will be threatened.

Family reunions are often an unhappy time for an obsessive person, because there he is not in control. Cousins and aunts and uncles and grand-mothers are meeting together, and nobody cares what the other person owns or knows or controls. The atmosphere is light and comfortable, but the chit-chat drives him up a wall. He is often the first to leave because it is difficult to pick out a role with that many familiar people around.

Role playing even extends to the obsessive person's closest relationships. It is one thing to think, *I am at work now, so I will act like a worker*. It is another matter when he says to himself, *I am a husband, so I must act like a husband*. This reduces even the most intimate relationship to mere performance. He kisses his wife and says "I love you" on schedule; he even brings flowers often enough to keep things in control. He is usually the last one to dicover that his wife is unhappy and his marriage is in trouble. He is not sufficiently in touch with her feelings or his own to know the true situation. More often than not the obsessive male refuses to believe that he is largely responsible for an unhappy marriage. He will even give you the facts to show that it is not his fault.

SLOWING DOWN THE TREADMILL

The Lord can use a willing person to help the obsessive individual grow toward emotional maturity. The key is to counter his rigidity and intellectualism with patience, understanding, and wise counsel. Here are a few specifics.

Listen in loving silence. The overstructured person talks and stays busy to avoid feeling. The first thing to do, then, is quite simple: do nothing. Listen to him and he will eventually run out of words. If you argue with him, you will only be increasing his mental activity. Let him run out of fuel, and he will begin to slow down on his own. If he knows that you accept him completely—even his highly structured approach to life— then the feelings will come.

Be prepared for him to experience some irrational fears. One of these may be the fear of going "crazy." As soon as an obsessive person experiences strong feelings, he thinks he is cracking up. As a rule of thumb, though, the obsessive person who feels as though he is going crazy is the one who never does.

The "crazy" person thinks *we* are crazy.

A nineteen-year-old schizophrenic told me during a counseling session that I was missing out on life and that I was completely out of touch with my world. She went on to say, "A few days ago some idiot tried to tell me I am a schizophrenic. That's ridiculous."

She was, in fact, a severely regressed schizophrenic who heard voices, saw angels and dinosaurs, and who believed that her mind was teaching her to fly an airplane. Yet she thought the rest of the world was abnormal.

Our obsessive friend will not crack up when he experiences feelings. He is a person who has been in touch with reality throughout life. His emotions are now coming to the surface and he cannot keep everything structured, so he is afraid. He is afraid of his feelings and the loss of control that results when he is in touch with himself.

One of my obsessive clients broke down some controls during therapy and started crying. In fact, he began to sob uncontrollably. It was good for him, because he had control and structure to spare. He cried and laughed, then cried and laughed again. At times he was so frightened that he wanted to grasp my arm and hang onto me. His emotions had taken over temporarily, and he did not have control of the situation. This experience, and others that followed, were good for him. Of course, not all obsessive persons will react this strongly to their feelings. Whatever his reaction, wait for your friend to feel, and expect his feelings to frighten him.

Point out his resistance to feelings. Tell him, in simple terms, about his efforts to avoid feeling.

For example, you might say, "You say you don't like the pastor's innovations in the worship service. What is it about a new situation that threatens you so much?" Or, "You have given me a very complete list of reasons why you dislike her. But tell me, what do you *feel* about her?" Or, "I wonder if this fast-driving pace is keeping you from facing some feelings that you do not want to deal with."

In each case you are making use of his preoccupation with facts and problem solving to help him grow. Do not tell him why he does what he does, because he will argue with you or reject your idea completely. Ask him, "Why?" His mind will begin to work on solutions to the problems caused by his rigidity.

You might have to remind your friend that although both of you know that he does not like a certain person, yet he treats this person as if they were on the best of terms. So you might say, "You seem to go out of your way to be nice to him. I wonder if he's threatening you."

At this point you might encounter the obsessive person's technique of "doing and undoing." He will give you five reasons why he does not like the person and then be smitten with guilt feelings because his conscience says he should not feel that way. So he neutralizes his negative comments and his guilt by giving you a list of good qualities. If he has made a negative statement, he may hurriedly retract it or qualify it. This demonstrates his ambivalence about things such as right and wrong, good and evil. This ambivalence is the result of his need to maintain perfect balance in his life. Ambivalence is, for example, loving and hating someone at the same time. One response to this is to say, "I sense that you are afraid of your angry feelings. If you are angry at someone who is important to you, it seems you are afraid you will hurt them or drive them away."

The point of this second step in counseling is to deal with feelings. The obsessive person will spend a lot of time revealing his rigid system of thought, but eventually the counselor will have the opportunity to say, "I know what you think, but how do you feel?"

Emphasize his need for interpersonal relationships. Point out his overemphasis of facts and ideas. Help him to understand the difference between being involved with ideas and being involved with people. He needs to see the forest; he already has the trees memorized. Share with him how the Lord loved people and took time for them. Show him from Scripture that Jesus expressed emotions such as love, anger, and sorrow. He prayed fervently to His Father and He wept. The way you treat your friend helps him to relate to others and invest in them as people rather than as objects. We need to love and accept those who cannot express their emotions, just as Christ did. When we face our needs and look to Jesus, He is there. He is patient and loving. Although He confronts us with our shortcomings, He is most eager to help us become the fully human persons He created us to be. We can do the same for others.

5

The Problem
of Hysterical Emotions

The Book of Ruth provides the background for studying our
next type of personality. The main character, Ruth, was a
well-balanced, loyal young woman who found grace in the eyes
of God. In the first chapter of Ruth we also meet her sister-in-
law, Orpah. This young woman can serve as an introduction to
the topic of hysterical emotions.

SETTING THE STAGE

Ruth and Orpah were the daughters-in-law of Naomi and
Elimelech. To escape famine, this Jewish couple had migrated
from Bethlehem to the land of Moab. After Elimelech died, his
sons, Mahlon and Chilion, married Moabite women, Orpah
and Ruth. As if enough tragedy had not already befallen the
family, both Mahlon and Chilion died ten years later. Naomi
was now in a foreign land without a husband and without
children; Ruth and Orpah, as well, were now widows.

In ancient Middle Eastern cultures, it was nearly impossible for a woman to subsist without a man to give her support, protection, and a family name. Hearing that the famine in Judah had ended, Naomi decided to return to her hometown. She encouraged Ruth and Orpah to return to their families in Moab:

> And Naomi said to her two daughters-in-law, "Go, return each of you to her mother's house. May the LORD deal kindly with you as you have dealt with the dead and with me. May the Lord grant that you may find rest, each in the house of her husband. Then she kissed them, and they lifted up their voices and wept. And they said to her, "No, but we will surely return with you to your people." But Naomi said, "Return, my daughters. Why should you go with me? Have I yet sons in my womb, that they may be your husbands? Return, my daughters! . . ." (Ruth 1:8-12).

Notice how the reactions of Ruth and Orpah differ:

> And they lifted up their voices and wept again; and Orpah kissed her mother-in-law, but Ruth clung to her. Then she [Naomi] said, "Behold, your sister-in-law has gone back to her people and her gods; return after your sister-in-law." But Ruth said, "Do not urge me to leave you or turn back from following you; for where you go, I will go, and where you lodge, I will lodge. Your people shall be my people, and your God, my God. Where you die, I will die, and there I will be buried. Thus may the Lord do to me, and worse, if anything but death parts you and me" (Ruth 1:14-17).

HISTORICAL FIRST: IN-LAWS GETTING ALONG!

Ruth and Orpah seemed to have a deep, loving attachment to their mother-in-law. In a profoundly moving scene, with all the men gone and the three women on the way to Bethlehem, Naomi suggested that her daughters-in-law go back to their families and look for another husband. "May the LORD grant that you may find rest, each in the house of her husband" (Ruth 1:9).

According to J. Sidlow Baxter in *Explore the Book* (Zondervan, 1960), the word *rest* signifies "safe shelter." He writes, "Now it was this fact that Naomi had in mind when she urged the return of Orpah and Ruth to seek safety, respect, and honor in their parents' homes, and then in the house of a husband." So "rest" here points toward marriage.

There are many Christian couples today who cannot imagine a marriage being restful; many of these people have more marital tension than they can handle. Nevertheless, Naomi said, in effect, "My children and husband are dead, and I am going back home. You will be better off looking for a family in your own culture."

Ruth and Orpah cried out in response to Naomi's two pleas that they return to their families. Both times they were overcome with emotion and wept. At this point we see the difference between Ruth and Orpah. Ruth followed through on emotions that were deeply felt. She added depth and character to the expression of her feelings.

Apparently Orpah's emotions were not as deep as Ruth's because she did not follow through and stay with Naomi. One moment she was kissing Naomi, weeping and promising to stay with her. The next moment she was gone. Orpah's actions and expressions of emotion point us to the expression of artificial feelings known as hysterical behavior.

TODAY'S HYSTERIC

The hysterical personality displays several major characteristics that help us to identify this personality type.

He expresses a great deal of shallow emotion. People like Orpah are vivid, exciting, and emotionally intense. Their thought processes and answers to questions, though, are not focused on reality. A typical exchange with a hysteric would go something like this:

"Tell me about your father."

"Oh, he's wham-bang!"

"Well, what's 'wham-bang'?"

"I don't really know. Every time I think of my father I just think of 'wham-bang.'"

This is obviously a quick, general, emotionally charged response that contains little true feeling or factual content. Consequently, we say that the hysterical person gives diffuse and often meaningless answers to life's questions. There is little chance of getting a factual response from the hysteric.

This person shows a severe lack of depth and sincerity. Something always seems to be awry; something is missing in his communications. For the person who is not trained in psychology, the hysteric's behavior can be a mystery that causes them and others a great deal of confusion and emotional pain.

He operates on the basis of spontaneous, emotional impression. The typical hysteric is prone to forget or avoid facts because he gets lost in a sea of immediate impressions.

Here is an example of the hysteric's susceptibility to immediate impression. You may have heard of the Rorschach test, an ink-blot test used by psychologists to study personality. It is a very useful tool, and really quite harmless. (I am of the opinion, by the way, that many things having to do with psychology are imagined to be something awesome and mysterious. Personality tests often fall into this category, and this is because they are not understood by untrained persons. This apprehension is unnecessary—tests such as the Rorschach are not the "bad guy.")

Let's imagine that most people consider one of the ink-blots to be a horse. The obsessive person would give facts about *why* he sees a horse, pointing out the body structure, color marks, whether or not it was shod—all the facts to validate his choice, without reporting any feeling. A conversation with the hysteric about the inkblot would go something like this:

"Oh, I hate horses. Get it out of here!"

"Why do you say it looks like a horse?"

"Well, it just does."

"Yes, but what is it about the blot that makes you think it is a horse?"

After getting frustrated, he will say, "I don't know, it just does. I don't want to look at it any more."

On another ink-blot, the obsessive person might see a skyscraper and its many offices. The hysteric, rather than deal with structure and a factual description, might turn the card upside down and report another vague first impression. Perhaps he would see a dark ocean.

He is incapable of concentration. To say it another way, he always needs to be inspired in order to function. The hysteric reacts to everyone else's emotion and is inspired and directed by it, almost as though he has no identity of his own. Whatever you are is what he will be. He acts on hunches and whims and has little or no intellectual curiosity.

His emotions are rarely integrated with accurate thinking, memory, or good judgment. Such avoidance of reality is often found in immature people who are about to be married. Their guiding principle is, Nothing matters but us two.

"That may be," we respond, "but don't you need a job and a place to live? Don't you need financial stability to get married? Two really *can't* live as cheaply as one."

"But we're in love, so every thing is going to work out. We don't have to worry."

This attitude of denying and ignoring reality sets them up for unhappiness and marital failure.

A hysteric will not remember his emotional outbursts from one week to the next. I administered the Rorschach test to a client one day and then again a week later. Most of her responses were emotional and impressionistic, but she gave me different answers on each test. Whereas an obsessive client would describe the ink-blot exactly as he had the week before, my hysterical client could not. This becomes clear from our conversation.

"Well, last week you saw the open jaws of a lion with a man's head inside. Show me the man's head today."

"Did I really see the head of a man last week? I don't remember that at all."

This refusal to integrate facts and demonstrate sound judgment is what causes the hysteric to be labeled "scatterbrained" or "flighty."

CHASING RAINBOWS

The characteristcs listed in the previous section cause many problems for the hysteric.

He does his best to avoid decision making. He will go to any length to stay away from facts. He operates totally on childlike, emotional responses because of his fear of growing up and facing a mature, adult world. Living is not always easy; it takes thought, planning, and responsibility to maintain an adequate life style and get along with others. The hysteric refuses to face the facts and says with Scarlett O'Hara, "I'll think about that tomorrow."

Most of us cannot understand why an adult who has been driving for thirty years would refuse to learn to read a road map. It is not that difficult a thing to master. One client put it this way: "My husband takes care of all that. When I'm ready to go, he shows me where I want to go. I don't want to read a map."

The point is, if she had learned to read the road map, she would be responsible to use the information and make correct decisions. The hysterical woman chooses instead to be controlled by an underlying need for dependence, and this reinforces her irresponsibility. Needless to say, her behavior here probably drives her husband up a tree! Unfortunately, it also undermines their communication with one another.

He guesses at solutions to problems. This can produce havoc in areas such as financial affairs and career decisions where responsible behavior is needed. The hysteric hopes that an inspiration of some sort will answer his difficulties, but this seldom happens. He quickly stops after dealing with appearances, rather than to ponder, plan, and be responsible for his feelings. Factual, structured thinking is difficult for him; a rational response is nearly impossible. The problem, again, is not that the hysteric lacks mental ability, but that he is so mired down in surface emotions that he does not take time to think.

He deliberately maintains a state of naiveté or ignorance about vital issues. This is merely another way to avoid responsibility for factual material. For example, some highly intelligent people who have been married for years remain unbelievably naive about human sexuality. In counseling, they do not have answers to simple questions about their sexual relationship. This is not a reflection on their intelligence; it is an amazing example of avoiding a highly charged issue that demands adult responsibility.

He is easily distracted by outside influences. The hysteric responds to the opinions of others, but not with his own ideas. For this reason, he will be concerned about *the* people to know, *the* night spots to frequent, *the* clothes to wear, *the* current book to read. . . . and the list goes on. Why? Because his immaturity causes intense concern for keeping pace with the interests and emotional state of others—to the detriment of his identity.

He is given to switching themes in serious conversation. When I point something out during therapy, the hysteric will jump tracks to another subject to avoid looking at the facts. An excited client might state, "Well, the thing I don't like about my husband is that he never phones when he's going to be late, and it makes me so upset I don't know what to do." If she and I figure out a way to remove the communication problem about her husband's schedule, she immediately jumps to another problem. It does not take long to realize that she is not interested in resolving problems. She is merely moving from one issue to the next to avoid dealing with the facts and her deeper feelings about them. The hysteric's emotions seem unreal and unconvincing to a mature person.

He relates to others in a theatrical style. Have you ever experienced a hysteric attempting to make a point? It was difficult to tell if he really had any feeling about what was upsetting him. His expressions and overly emotional statements probably seemed hollow, as if the emotions were more important than the issue.

This overdramatic voice, which suggests the speaker is experiencing pain and torment, often drives people away. Although this mannerism sounds unconvincing to a person with insight, we should not be too hard on these folks. Hysterics are truly unaware they are acting. For that reason, some of them do very well in Hollywood.

I counseled a movie star once, a man who did not know who he really was. "When I'm playing a hard guy," he said, "I feel tough and mean all the time. When I'm in a romantic role, I fall in love with every woman who comes along. I can't seem to separate the actor-me from the person-me. I feel like I am always on stage and have to act all the time instead of just living and being happy." Fortunately, this was a mature statement by a hysteric who had made great progress in therapy. Before we had talked together, he had been unaware that he was always acting instead of relating with people.

For the hysteric the world is a stage. They feel much like characters in a romance, where everything falls into place magically and everyone lives happily ever after. The problem with this system is twofold. First, if life is a fairy tale, then no matter what they do, everything should be OK in the long run. Obviously, this leads to irresponsible behavior. Secondly, the truth is that life is *not* a fairy tale. The hysteric often comes to a rude awakening when things do not work out. His glimpses of reality are a bucket of cold water in the face!

The hysterical woman is often sexually unresponsive or even frigid. Her lack of emotional depth makes her incapable of sexual fulfillment. She is always looking for Prince Charming on a white horse, and she is oblivious to the flaws of each new person she is attracted to. She is "in love with love."

Occasionally a hysteric will "fall in love with" her therapist and proceed to list fantastic qualities and character traits— those wonderful things that caused her to be swept off her feet. However, the traits she finds most lovable about him may be characteristics he has never had and never will possess. She is living and loving in an internal fantasy world. She has no rational basis for assessing whether the therapist possesses the qualities she lists.

The hysteric projects responsibility onto others. Imagine a Christian marriage made up of a hysterical woman and an obsessive man. The woman may express hostility at her husband: she screams, and sobs, and scratches, and threatens to commit suicide. He decides he has had enough. He replies, "I'm leaving!" Because Prince Charming never divorces Cinderella in fairy tales, the wife cries, "I don't understand why you are doing this to me." It is as if she is saying subconsciously,

> *I don't really mean the things I say, so what I say doesn't really count. Even if I am coming through really strong, you shouldn't take me seriously because I don't mean what I am saying.*

The hysterical person does not want to be responsible for what he says and does.

The hysteric does not regard his emotional outbursts as something he has really felt. He considers his violent feelings to be a mysterious seizure or something that has come over him as a result of someone else's actions. Of course, this is immature and irresponsible thinking.

The hysteric might attempt to explain his acting out by saying: "I really don't know why I said the things I did. I don't know where it came from. It's as though something hit me and it just came out." The hysteric's assessments and judgments are not rooted in firm convictions or understanding.

OPPOSITES ATTRACT

Although both the hysteric and the obsessive person tend toward extremes, hysterical and obsessive behavior differ greatly. A brief comparison will help us understand each personality better.

Usually, the obsessive person is not difficult to understand. He remembers facts and figures. An obsessive person will come for therapy and say, "I don't know why I am here, because I know everything that went wrong and why I am the way I am." Then he will proceed to give a list of significant events in his childhood, including at what age each occurred and what effect each had on his development!

Obsessive persons are great with facts and data, but they are not in touch with their feelings. The person with a healthy blend of facts and feelings will be more well adjusted than the hysteric or the obsessive person. If the obsessive person could feel more and the hysteric could think more, both would be better off.

Often the hysterical woman is attracted to and marries an obsessive man. A little reflection and insight shows us why. The hysteric tends to come "unglued" easily. This accounts for the most common use of the term *hysterical*—"Having a tendency toward uncontrolled violent emotional outbreaks." The overly emotional woman in our example prefers to "gush"—to express herself through every available channel. From deep within her comes the thought, *If I can marry a man who is structured, who has everything under control, I will have found the missing ingredient.* She identifies with his high degree of organization because she is so unorganized, and he maintains control in their marriage. This symbiotic relationship often backfires, however, and this is one of the most common problem marriages encountered by the professional counselor.

Although the hysteric is usually "object related" (a person who interacts with other people and their feelings, attitudes, and values), his relationships with other people are often unsatisfying. In the example above, the marriage runs into difficulty because the woman does not receive the emotional input that she needs in order to continue to function as a hysteric. Her obsessive husband is extremely punctual and businesslike. He does not express his emotions; he is caught up in his career and in his intellectual approach to life.

Jim comes home to the newspaper, the TV, or his hobbies and does not look for opportunities to share his feelings with his wife. At the same time, Mary needs to hear that she is beautiful. Jim is tired and wants to be left alone while he watches the ball game. Mary feels like the love-starved wife who has been cheated out of everything she wanted in life.

At this point you may be asking, Why would an obsessive man marry a hyperemotional woman? It is because he is rigid and does not feel much. Because his life is so structured, he marries a gushy, emotional gadfly who needs to be around people. He seeks to live out his repressed emotions through her. However, because she is so disorganized and nonintellectual, he becomes more and more "uptight" with her scatter-brained behavior. This leads to the hostile attacks that put marriages on the rocks. Jim gets angry at Mary because she is not logical, and she flies to pieces. Next step, of course, is to see a good psychologist or marriage counselor to work on the problem.

THE SOCIAL CHAMELEON

Here, just as with the other personality types in this book, not many persons are pure hysterics. Very few people are locked into a single style of relating to the world. It is dangerous, and certainly not helpful, to use a psychological diagnosis to label a person, especially when one is untrained. Every so often, though, a therapist comes across a client who fits the textbook description of a personality type almost perfectly. One of my clients, whom we will call Andrea, had many personality characteristics of the hysteric.

Andrea was one of the most popular girls at school, and much of her activity was geared to maintaining that position. She was flirtatious and lively; she gave great parties and, in general, she insisted on having a good time. Her relationships and her communication with others were superficial and overly emotional. On one occasion, she insisted that her boyfriend escort her to a pep rally and football game. "You just have to be there with me," she cried. "All my friends are going, and it will ruin my whole school year if we don't go." This type of emotional exaggeration and overreaction was frequent.

Andrea operated on impressions and was subject to the influence of others. Her moods were unpredictable and they changed quickly. She could be alone in the house and crying one moment, and then shut off the tears and smile as the doorbell rang. Before the visitor drove off she would be in tears again. The feelings she was expressing were superficial and transparent.

Andrea appeared to be in the forefront of social activity, but she was actually following the lead of others. Her high school friends were sexually promiscuous, and she followed their example. After she graduated, church became the center of her social life, so she experienced an immediate "super spiritual" revival of faith and became, you guessed it, director of social activities. Even her vocabulary changed overnight. She began to use "brother" and "sister" to refer to other people.

At a Christian college, Andrea rose quickly to prominence in student government, only to leave school after a year. She became engaged by way of correspondence. So she married a man she had dated less than six weeks.

In all of this, Andrea demonstrated instability and a tendency to conform, as well as the ill-founded belief that she could marry a near stranger and have an instantly happy marriage. Andrea and people like her are emotional chameleons; they change direction and their feelings shift as soon as the world around them changes. An unending chain of influences, which stimulate a great deal of emotion, carry the hysteric through life on a shallow current of feelings. These shallow feelings prevent him from experiencing life fully.

HOW TO HELP THE HYSTERIC

Somewhere in the shadows of his youth the dependent, hyperemotional hysteric developed a block or hindrance to his emotional growth. To understand him, we need to ask questions such as: "Why is he afraid to take on responsibility and trust his own judgment? Why is she afraid to learn to read a road map? Why is he afraid to grow up and be independent?"

I sometimes use a journey across the U.S. continent to illustrate the concept of blocks to emotional growth. If a pioneer family set out from Virginia by covered wagon and made it all the way to Kansas, we would call that progress. Suppose that twenty miles into Colorado they were attacked by Indians and narrowly escaped. They might continue their journey or be scared into heading back to Kansas. If they are frightened enough, they will live the rest of their lives in the strongest, safest fort they can find.

Immature personalities are those who stay in Kansas or Colorado, or those who never even find the courage to leave Virginia. Anxiety and the fear of personal growth are the two primary reasons why people cling to an inadequate behavior system. The hysteric has, in a sense, locked himself inside a fort whose walls are made of irresponsible, gushy emotionalism. He is afraid to think rationally and to deal responsibly with life because that means growth. It means moving toward California and facing the Indians again. The counselor can help to remove or ease the trauma and fear that the hysterical person experienced early in his life, so that he can continue his growth toward maturity.

The hysteric's life style may seem colorful and lively, but he is not happy. His personality has no depth, and he does not feel like a person. Often the hysteric will be plagued by a problem called agoraphobia—the fear of open places.

One of my clients became terrified whenever he thought about taking a vacation and getting away from Los Angeles. He was quite wealthy and could have lived anywhere he wanted. But any time he got more than a hundred miles out of town, he would be overcome by feelings and have to call just to hear my voice. We even set up a time for him to call me every day from a ski resort so that he could allow himself to continue his vacation in Utah. He desperately needed the structure that his dependence on me provided.

While in town, the familiar buildings and freeways kept him feeling safe and secure. Los Angeles was his fort. But flying to another state or driving through the desert caused his world to crumble. His attacks of anxiety terrified him, but through the process of personal growth in therapy he has gradually learned to deal with the problem on his own.

Occasionally he still feels anxious or fearful when he travels, but now he uses his thought processes to help him control these feelings. He thinks about the problem and about some solutions we have worked out together. He reported to me recently, "I was just about to do some water skiing at the lake when I felt like I was coming unglued. But I remembered that when I had felt the same way once before, I called you and we talked together. So I applied what you told me then and I found I could handle the situation."

The structure that was once external, his dependence on me, he was able to make a part of himself. He was able to feel, but he was also able to use his thought processes to put things together. This personal growth and mature behavior is our goal in working with the hysteric.

The hysteric and impulsive personalities have much in common. The hysteric is irresponsible in his feelings; the impulsive person is irresponsible about his actions. Both find it difficult to control and integrate feelings. Some of the same techniques used to help the impulsive person will be useful in relating with the hysteric. However, we must first make a distinction.

The impulsive person "acts out"; that is, he does not care about the results of a specific action or about the future. He does whatever he pleases without regard for society. The hysteric, on the other hand, "acts in." He uses an emotional state, which is normally internal, to relate to the outer world. His behavior—the crying, the demands, and the manipulation of others—is the result of a lack of control over his feelings. His emotional state is dumped on others without restraint. Acting in is the lesser of two evils because it is the expression of emotions rather than a physical action. However, the hysteric does need to learn to think before emoting. There are several things we can do to help him.

Set limits to control acting in. Help him to make sure his brain is in gear before his mouth is in motion. Use a calm, logical, and precise manner when you talk to him. Gently keep him on the subject at hand so that he cannot jump from feeling to feeling and from problem to problem. Be direct, yet supportive as you encourage him to think, to reason, and to face the facts; this will go a long way in helping an overemotional person.

Teach the hysteric to introspect. Introspection is the ability to understand why we feel the way we do and how these feelings developed. Rather than the two of you discussing every aspect of his emotional reactions, encourage him to look at the facts behind his feelings. Help him ask questions about his emotions. He knows *what* he feels; he needs to learn *why* he feels.

The hysteric needs to integrate his emotional life with rational thought processes. In short, one of the most beneficial things one can do for an overly emotional person is to teach him to think. He needs to learn to think, not just about his feelings, but about the world around him and his responsibilities.

Help him structure responsibility for his life. If he needs to learn to read a road map, gently but firmly refuse to allow him to depend on you to give him directions. However, be supportive of his efforts to learn map reading.

There are many ways to teach him responsibility for his life. Show him how to balance and maintain a checking account. Help him to develop a budget to avoid fad-controlled buying. Encourage him to think about how others might be reacting to his overt expression of feelings. Above all, help him to see that he alone is responsible for his emotional outbursts and conduct.

As stated previously, hysterical persons are often sexually naive. Therefore, urge him to take full responsibility for his sexual identity. The human body is a miraculous creation of God, and it is good for us to know how and why we function sexually. There are books on the market that discuss human sexuality from a biblical perspective. Encourage him to read them. Be available to discuss the Christian view of sexuality. He needs to be aware of the sexual aspect of his God-given nature and how it affects his relationships with others.

Personal and spiritual growth is God's purpose for each of us. Paul writes: "And do not be conformed to this world, but be transformed by the renewing of your mind" (Rom. 12:2). As we grow, we can help others. The hysteric needs the calm, consistent love that encourages him to use his thought processes. Remember that in the earliest years of life emotion dominates over intellect. Generally speaking, little children are more prone to spontaneous, uncontrolled expression of feelings than adults. The hysteric is very childlike and dependent because he is continually being stalked by fear. He uses his emotions to maintain a relationship of dependence on those around him.

He has never fully experienced love as the Bible describes it: "There is no fear in love; but perfect love casts out fear" (1 John 4:18). The deadlock of fear will be broken as you help him to make use of his thought processes while still assuring him that you care about him. Then the hysteric will begin to integrate his intellect and his emotions. He needs to learn that "God has not given us a spirit of timidity, but of power and love and discipline [sound judgment]" (2 Tim. 1:7).

6

Heman in the
Valley of Depression

It strikes us all, this thing called depression. We all get the blues once in a while. Everybody has their down days, and a certain amount of depression is normal even in the healthiest personality. It is only when one cannot free himself from depression that the problem becomes serious. Lengthy or severe depression is cause for alarm.

The 1970s have been called the decade of depression. Across our country and around the world, depression is an increasing phenomenon. Merely reading about the subject causes us to be more in touch with our own feelings. You may even think that depression is a depressing topic, but there is light at the end of the tunnel. Depression is common, and we do need to know how and why it occurs; but this understanding will equip us to help our friends who are suffering.

In the past man's understanding and treatment of depression was poor. Sometimes the patient was spun around on a rapidly revolving chair in order to drive out depression and the bad spirits. At one time it was also thought that high blood pressure was the cause of depression, so blood was drained from the person to reduce the amount of fluid in his cardiovascular system. An even more bizarre treatment was to drill a hole in the skull to relieve pressure.

In modern times, we know that depression is primarily a mental and emotional problem, not physical. As we shall see, it is the "disease of loss." To get a biblical perspective, we will examine Psalm 88, one of the most melancholy passages in Scripture.

A MAN WITHOUT HOPE

Psalm 88 was written by a man named Heman. Perhaps the name is new to you, but in fact there are two men by that name in the Bible. One was the grandson of Samuel the prophet. He had fourteen sons and three daughters. With that big a family, we might expect to read that this was the Heman who was depressed!

This man's family was made up of musicians. First Chronicles 25 describes their ministry of music, as well as that of two other families. All of these people were trained in singing praises to the Lord, and they served in the time of King David. There were 288 vocal and instrumental performers in all.

The other Heman was a very wise man, and he is mentioned in 1 Kings 4:31. Here it states that the wisdom of Solomon was greater than that of several wise men, and Heman is included in this group. Although the Bible commentaries are not in total agreement, most indicate that this is the man who wrote Psalm 88.

Many of the psalms written by David, the well-known shepherd-king of Israel, contain helpful, comforting words. Yet in the midst of these psalms is a song of pain and darkness and depression. Psalm 88 is a lamentation written by a man we know little about. Its despondent chorus ends without the slightest hint of comfort or joy. Within its lines are the painful statements of a man who felt hopeless and alone.

SONG OF SORROW

> O LORD, the God of my salvation,
> I have cried out by day and in the night before Thee (v. 1).

The psalm begins with words filled with emotion. It sounds as if this man is staggering under a load of pressure and crying for relief. This tells us something about the nature of depression.

Depression is actually a defense against anxiety. It is a reaction against the fear and stress of trying to cope in an unfriendly world. If either the world outside or one's emotions are too threatening, a person may repress his feelings and become depressed. This takes place without the person being consciously aware of it, of course.

Tears are a wonderful gift of God for dealing with stress, and at times they also accompany depression. Tears help to express anger or shame or sadness, and they help to relieve depression. Severely depressed people have been known to cry for hours or even days.

Heman cried out to the Lord both day and night. His deep depression did not lift; it was with him around the clock.

> Let my prayer come before Thee;
> Incline Thine ear to my cry! (v. 2).

Heman said in effect, "Lord, I feel so terribly alone. I feel all tied up in knots. I don't know what to do. Please come to me; reach out and help me." This is the language of the depressed person. It expresses the pure dependence of one who is withdrawn and crying for help. In the same way, when we are dejected and alone, we will often phone a friend or reach out in some way. We all need answers, encouragement, and support. Heman turned to God for relief, but it is obvious that at the same time he felt distant from Him. Heman's song is a song of sorrow.

CONFLICT AND EXHAUSTION

The depressed person experiences tremendous conflict. In the words of Heman:

> For my soul has had enough troubles (v.3).

A depressed person usually feels overly guilty, and he is sensitive and worries constantly. He thinks that anything pleasureful must be wrong, so he punishes himself with unnecessary guilt. He thinks to himself, *If I balance out my pleasure side with a guilty side, everything will be OK*. This neurotic thinking leaves him paralyzed and he collapses into an emotional heap. His conflicts literally immobilize him.

Heman continues,

> And my life has drawn near to Sheol (v. 3).

Heman seems preoccupied with death; it seems as if he felt he was about to die. He expresses conflict too great for him to handle. His mind and heart are spent. In simple terms, he is completely exhausted. In the same way, the depressed person entertains morbid thoughts about death and dying. I have worked with clients who would sit at various tombstones for ten or more hours a week.

Heman continues,

> I am reckoned among those who go down to the pit;
> I have become like a man without strength,
> Forsaken among the dead,
> Like the slain who lie in the grave. . . (vv. 4-5)

In a sense, the depressed person identifies with those who are cut off from the living. His feelings are similar to a death wish.

There is a life drive in each of us. We want to live. When asked why they want to live, most people will reply that they want to accomplish or experience something they have not yet realized. We want to fulfill our dreams. We want to be and do all that we can.

The depressed person has lost so much hope that his will to live is at least temporarily lessened. He feels as if nothing will work out right again. It makes no difference to him what happens. In other words, his mood determines how he feels. His mood affects everything he does; it even colors his ideas and his thinking process. It is as if he is saying to himself, *I feel lousy, so my married life is lousy. My job is terrible. World conditions are hopeless. What's the point? Why bother?*

Heman expresses this mood. He is saying, "I feel drawn down to the bottom of the pit. I'm not only thinking about death—I'm as good as gone. My strength is all used up and I don't think I can make it any more." A truly depressed person has little energy left for combating his moods. Conflicts and feelings seem so overwhelming that he cannot find the strength to cope.

Did Heman add, "But at least I feel close to you, Lord"? Hardly! He felt cut off from God. His cry continues,

> . . . Whom Thou dost remember no more,
> And they are cut off from Thy hand (v. 5).

It is easy to see why a depressed person has so much trouble praying. The problem may be mental rather than spiritual. He is fatigued. He is in anguish and his mind is full of conflict. He has wracked his brain to no avail and is so emotionally exhausted that he cannot make any progress. This emotional fatigue can easily block effective prayer.

Emotional conflict is also much more tiring than physical stress. It entails more suffering. A young friend of mine is training to become a Christian psychologist for this reason. He served as a medical corpsman with a Marine Corps helicopter squadron in Vietnam. Although he originally entered college with the goal of becoming a medical doctor, his military experience led him to change his vocation. The reason? He found that although the physical pain and damage of combat injuries was terrible, the mental anguish of war was greater.

Firsthand experience convinced him that emotional pain and suffering are more severe than physical pain. For this reason, he is learning how to work with people who hurt inside.

It is usually harder to relax and sleep after mental stress than after a physical workout. However, this inability to sleep is not always true for the depressed person. Some of them want to escape from life by sleeping all the time. The problem is one of extremes—too much sleep or none at all.

SELF-MADE STANDARDS

Heman reveals more of the feelings of depressed people.

> Thou hast put me in the lowest pit,
> In dark places, in the depths.
> Thy wrath has rested upon me,
> And Thou hast afflicted me with all Thy waves (vv. 6-7).

This suggests some of the obstacles that all of us, and especially the depressed person, can put in the way of our own emotional growth.

A severe conscience can lead to depression. An overactive conscience can make the depressed person feel constantly guilty. This depression can be so severe that he feels everyone is criticizing him. He fears that others are talking about him and putting him down. This paranoid fear is even injected into his spiritual life. This explains why Heman blamed God for his troubles and his feelings.

The Lord does allow us to go through hard times for our own good. There is no strength without exercise. There is no growth without pain. When we find purpose and meaning in our trials and suffering, we are able to work through it. We become stronger and healthier and more able to help someone else. Heman could not face his troubles, so he projected responsibility onto God. The natural consequence of blaming God for our troubles is seen in verses 6 and 7—Heman felt that God did not love him any more.

A depressed Christian often fears he has lost his salvation. He feels alone and separated from God. As a young pastor I usually ended my sermons with an invitation to receive Christ. One man responded to the invitation nine Sunday evenings in a row. Attending church cheered him up and he felt close to God each Sunday, but he was depressed the rest of the week. He feared he had lost his salvation along the way. The emotional isolation he experienced was transferred to his feelings about God. This caused him to doubt God's love and his own salvation. He needed to be reassured each Sunday in order to have peace of mind.

Depressed persons in the church have a problem believing they are still on God's side. It is hard to believe you are accepted when you *feel* worthless. Heman's words, "And Thou hast afflicted me with all Thy waves," indicate strong feelings about God's standards. An overactive conscience causes the depressed person to struggle with all the things he thinks he should be doing, and his expectations are so high that no one is able to help him.

Many pastors ask the same question about some of their most solid church members. "Why is it that so many of my best people feel like failures—the ones who are always well prepared, who do a good job teaching and fulfilling their responsibilities? Why do they always want to quit because they think they aren't good enough?" Perhaps it is because these people create such high standards for themselves that they can never live up to them. This can only lead to depression.

These self-made standards of perfection that seem to us to be from God actually come between God and us. Jesus declared: "Therefore you are to be perfect, as your heavenly Father is perfect" (Matt. 5:48). This does not mean that we must be without mistakes or must somehow instantly become as holy as God. It means, rather, to be fulfilled, to be mature. It encourages us to be all we can be by the grace of God. When we construct impossible standards for ourselves, we are merely resorting to a self-made law. Jesus came to give us abundant life, not depression.

The result of demanding too much of ourselves is the feeling that God does not approve of us. We begin to feel that He is cutting us off. If we think we cannot measure up for God, then we also feel unworthy of the love and appreciation of others. Heman speaks of this:

> Thou hast removed my acquaintances far from me;
> Thou hast made me an object of loathing to them . . . (v. 8).

The depressed person generally has a bad self-concept. It is as if he is saying, "If you know too much about me, you won't like me. And I really am worthless, so don't bother to get too close." The hostility he believed was coming from God and other people, he now turns in on himself. He hates himself. He has no reason to live. He thinks, *Why should anybody like me? I'm just a horrible wretch*. He feels like he is an undesirable person.

ANGRY ISOLATION

The next line of the psalm shows why Heman felt cut off from God and people:

> . . . I am shut up and cannot go out (v. 8).

This brings to mind what psychologists call *introversion* (the act of directing one's interest inward or to things within the self). Each of us has a certain amount of emotional drive, and this emotional energy is usually directed toward another person. For example, the reason we get together for fellowship and even the reason we marry is because we need to invest this energy in another human being. A person who has experienced considerable pain may invest his emotional drive in property or animals, but generally we seek out people to love.

The depressed person feels cut off from others, so he turns his emotional investment back into himself. He lives in mental isolation. Like the snail, he withdraws into his shell and lives by himself. He can be lonely in the midst of people, and he pulls back from those who try to help him.

A woman I had been counseling called me when she was very depressed. She said, "I really shouldn't be bothering you. I know it's your day off. You should be with your family instead of talking to me. I shouldn't be taking up your time. Why would you want to be bothered with someone as messed up as I am? I just felt like I wanted to take my own life so I thought I'd better call. I'm just sorry I got in your way like this."

Note the lack of self-worth here. She actually believed she was not worth my time! Her husband got on the phone and explained, "She's just been closing up completely into herself lately. She doesn't talk. She doesn't want to share anything. Seems like she's brooding all the time—a lot of strong emotions there, but nothing seems to come out." She was in fact withdrawing further and further into herself.

Although it is not easily detected, it is a fact that depressed people harbor a great deal of anger. Note the buried anger in the words of Heman:

> My eye has wasted away because of affliction;
> I have called upon Thee every day, O LORD;
> I have spread out my hands to Thee. (v. 9).

It seemed to Heman that God was far away. He might have said, "He may not care at all. He's too busy with other people. I probably don't even matter to Him. Hey, God! I'm calling out to You and You're still far away."

A depressed person may not show it on the outside, but he is angry and cannot get it out. If he did express his hostility, his feelings of worthlessness and of being evil would reappear. His only recourse is to hold it in. This internalized anger only increases depression and feelings of "bad self."

A deeply depressed person can love you one day and hate you the next, simply because his anger vacillates. Generally speaking, though, the depressed stance is, "I am horrible, but you are a good person. The world is good, but I am bad."

Heman continues to express veiled anger at God:

> Wilt Thou perform wonders for the dead?
> Will the departed spirits rise and praise Thee?
> Will Thy loving kindness be declared in the grave,
> Thy faithfulness in the place of destruction?
> Will Thy wonders be made known in the darkness?
> And Thy righteousness in the land of forgetfulness? (vv. 10-12).

His is the expression of one who has no hope; he feels that God is holding out on him. He asks, "Do I have to die before you do something, God?"

One eye-opening truth about anger is that we often transfer anger from its source to an easier target. The classic example of this is the "I hate my mother-in-law" syndrome. It feels safer to hate an in-law than one's own mother. This psychological trick is called *displacement*—we displace our feelings about one person onto another. The depressed person who expresses anger toward God is actually displacing the hostility he feels toward someone else, but cannot face.

Because the depressed person's conscience constantly hammers away at him, nothing you say or do will convince him that he is a worthwhile person. His conscience not only pronounces continual judgment, it also acts as a screen through which the depressed person sifts all comments. If you condemn him, his conscience will agree with you. If you attempt to compliment him, the message will not get through to him. He will not accept positive statements about himself, no matter how true they are. Therefore, even when he is among friends, the depressed person will continue to feel alone and unworthy.

This isolated feeling causes the deeply depressed person to be angry at the people who want to be close to him. He blames them for his problem but refuses to allow them to help solve it. He keeps them at a distance with his introversion, his overactive conscience, and his feeling of unworthiness.

Heman and those like him may feel that God has cast them off. Heman cried:

> O Lord, why dost Thou reject my soul?
> Why dost thou hide Thy face from me? (v. 14).

The truth is, God desires union with all men who will turn to Him. The depressed person shuts himself off so that he cannot sense the presence of God; this does not mean God is not there.

God's constant availability is well illustrated in the following story. An old farmer and his wife were bouncing down a country road in their old pickup. The wife was sitting on the far side of the cab, knitting as her husband drove.

Noticing the distance between them, she turned to ask, "Why don't we sit close together—the way we did when we first got married?"

He thought for a moment and then drawled, "Well, I didn't move."

That's how our Lord is. He does not move away from us. When there is a gap and we cannot feel His presence, guess who moved? Fortunately, depression is not a hopeless condition. No problem is insurmountable when we understand it and face it with His help. In the next chapter we will discuss some of the causes of depression and what to do about it.

7

The Decade
of Depression

Our society has been the setting for ever-increasing depression over the past few years. There is no question that many Americans are discouraged and confused. Others are apathetic. To whom shall we turn? The consensus is that the government and those in positions of power have let us down. People seem to be saying, "I'm not a Democrat. I'm not a Republican. I don't even know if I'm an Independent."

There are many things that are causing depression and the loss of values. Our social standards are in a constant state of flux. One of my clients shared with me, "I work in a law office. I swear that the whole place is going to pieces. One attorney is cheating on his wife, and she has a boyfriend. One of the secretaries lives with her boyfriend and she's pregnant. Two of the other women are homosexual and live together. I've had three different lovers myself this week, and now I feel really lost. My medical doctor told me I was depressed and that I needed to work someplace where people at least have their values straightened out. I'm depressed because everything is changing and nothing is dependable any more."

It seems the problems are endless. The public debt is astronomical. We are faced with pollution, fuel shortages, and rising crime rates. The cost of even a modest home can be exorbitant, and newlyweds must cope with heavy financial burdens as they begin a family these days.

Our country has suffered loss of esteem in a war that divided the national spirit. In a sense we lost our feeling of being an unbeatable military power. Thousands of families lost fathers and sons. Many people were haunted by the question, "Is my boy still alive somewhere?" The boiling rage and frustrated anger of the counterculture of the 60s have been reabsorbed into society. This internalization of an angry force might affect the nation just as it does the individual. We are witnessing the results of the forces of loss in our country.

The 1970s, and perhaps the early 1980s, will be remembered as an era of depression. The unspoken question that dominated the '76 presidential election campaign was, "Is there any hope?" There *is* hope, but it does not lie in the hands of the nation or the government. The solution belongs to the individuals who determine to regain a sense of balance and positive perspective in life. Because deep depression must be dealt with on an individual basis, we need to look at the specific things which make some people more susceptible to the emotional malady.

WHAT BRINGS ON THE BLUES?

There are common causes for periodic depression in people who are basically healthy. The first of these is a loss of love. If a romance breaks up or a friend mistreats you, you feel down for a while; but the healthy person bounces back soon enough. He renews the friendship that was strained for a moment or looks for a new girl friend. He continues to invest his emotional energy in a healthy manner.

A blow to our self-esteem may also cause depression. The loss of power, prestige, property, or good looks can bring a few down days. Most of us like to think highly of ourselves. We need a little self-respect to balance the blows from the world around us. However, if our bubble bursts and we lose something that contributes to our self-esteem, we take a nose dive. Usually we are back in stride in a short while, because we have the strength to work through the disappointment.

A frequent cause of depression is the problem of "success neurosis." It is quite common in our achievement-oriented society. For example, a man may get a raise and feel depressed about it. It is a topsy-turvy sort of phenomenon; most of us would be happy to get more money. Another example is the person who is in good physical shape, with a successful career and happy marriage. Even the future looks secure, but he says, "I don't know why I'm so depressed."

Success depression can come from a pause in a hectic, striving life style. A young client of mine was in student government in college and an honor student as well as being a part-time youth pastor. He was also active socially. He was busy, to say the least, and frequently complained about his demanding schedule. "Yet," he said, "when Friday afternoon comes along and the work is done at school, I always get depressed. I have to run out and find something to do to feel OK again."

Poor reality testing is another cause of the disappointment that characterizes depression. If we insist on painting castles in the air, we will be disillusioned when reality gets in the way. Castles in the air are not bad, mind you, if you can put a foundation under them. But if we picture ourselves as greater than we are, we are in for a fall. If we picture God as under our control and riding in our pocket, we are in for a big surprise.

EARLY CAUSES

Depression, then, is the disease of loss. If your new car is smashed up while parked on the street, you might suddenly feel both angry and depressed. You lost something of value. If your home burned down, you would feel depressed for the same reason. Depression is normal in the life of every human being. We all lose people or possessions that we value. It is a part of living and cannot be helped. Although temporary depression occurs periodically in everyone's life, chronic depression has roots in early childhood.

Somewhere in the first few years of life, the chronically depressed person experienced a real or imagined loss that was too severe for their infant ego to handle. Therefore, day-to-day occurrences that most of us would take in stride send this unfortunate person over the brink into serious depression. What are some of these early childhood losses?

The loss of one or both parents by death or divorce. This is the first and most obvious cause. This incredible blow to the dependent child is enough to prevent the ego from ever learning to deal with smaller losses.

The "duty-bound mother." If mom is loving and accepting but views mothering as nothing but hard work, the child may experience deep feelings of rejection. He will lose the foundation of unity between himself and his parent. He will then turn his mother's preoccupation with duty in on himself. The result is guilt and a self-condemning sense of duty toward the mother who in fact loved him a great deal. Because he can never measure up to what he subconsciously feels is expected of him, the child lives with guilt and failure.

Abrupt weaning. If a baby is abruptly weaned from bottle or breast to a glass at about six months of age, he will experience a significant loss of love. Babies feel loved when they are warm, dry, fed, and held. Body contact and the security of a soft, warm source of food are very important to the infant. When he loses the breast and the warm cuddling that is a part of both breast and bottle feeding, he loses love.

The birth of a sibling. In this frequent early cause of chronic depression the older child suddenly feels left out of the picture when his brother or sister is born. He tries to regain mother's full attention by "growing up" and improving himself, but nothing seems to happen. He develops the attitude, *I am bad or else mother would still love me*. The real or imagined loss of mother's love and the blow to his self-esteem are major setbacks in the ego development of the child. He is a prime target for recurring depression in adulthood.

WHAT YOU DON'T KNOW CAN HURT YOU

Although some of the roots of chronic depression are quite obvious, there are also causes that are not so apparent. We all have parts of our personality structure we are totally unaware of, and these subconscious mechanisms influence us more than we realize. Some people are more vulnerable to depression than others simply because of their subconscious fears and desires. Among the more significant underlying causes are:

The threat of loss. A person who has experienced the repeated threat of losing a love object will become depressed at the slightest hint of loss. Consider the child whose mother says, "If you don't clean your room, I'll give you away." Here is another saying that has a devastating effect on children: "I love you when you're good, but not when you're bad."

Inconsistent parental standards. This inconsistency influences the child's ego development and his later susceptibility to depression. Fluctuating standards only serve to confuse the child. It is as if the parent is saying, "I said no last week, but you can do it now if you want." An example is the parent who instructs his children never to lie and then says, "Go to the door and tell that salesman I'm not home."

Excessive parental standards frequently are a forerunner to chronic depression. When parental standards are too high, the child cannot meet their expectations. His only recourse is to keep trying and failing, and this leads to excessive guilt and depression. I know of one couple, for example, who expected their two-year-old to function as well at the dinner table as an adult. Severe parental standards rob the child of hope and encouragement. If he is scolded for C's in school, without his A's being mentioned, he will soon give up in defeat.

A subconscious desire to be taken care of. The need to be babied can be carried over from childhood. The depressed person often becomes very childlike and expects you to solve his problem for him. If you confront him with growing up or facing responsibility, he may withdraw even further. It is not uncommon for this person to stay curled up in bed with the covers over his head. This position, which reminds us of the security of the child in the womb, symbolizes the feelings of the depressed person.

SYMPTOMS

Most of the symptoms of depression are well known, since we all feel down once in a while. However, the intensity of the symptoms varies according to the severity of the depression.

A depressed person feels lonely, moody, lost, deserted, and abandoned. He also worries about his physical health. Headaches, gastro-intestinal discomfort, and backaches are accompanied by fatigue and lack of sleep. There is usually a loss of appetite, and his sex drive is much less intense.

As depression increases, the sufferer becomes irritable and short-tempered. He withdraws even further, losing interest in work and pleasure. He feels inferior and unworthy and the future seems hopeless. His paranoid fear of punishment and rejection becomes more apparent as his load of guilt increases.

Unfortunately the depressed person sets people up to hate him. He expects rejection, and therefore he functions in a way that makes it happen. When rejection occurs, the depression increases, and so he has come full circle.

Many of depression's victims are society's most useful people. They are hard-working, reliable, conscientious individuals who are serious about their work. These responsible people have high intellectual ability and a great capacity for achievement. Although they often have attained high social status, they make excessive demands of themselves. These unrealistic expectations cause internal and external loss, which results in guilt and depression. Constant brooding and second-guessing *(I'm not doing enough)* rob these people of the peace of mind and happiness they deserve.

COUNSELING THE DOWNHEARTED

Here are some practical suggestions for helping someone who is depressed.

Allow him to talk out all of his feelings. The depressed person must be listened to. However, depression causes him to turn inward, so you may find it difficult to get your depressed friend to talk. When he talks it out with you, though, pent-up feelings are shared and emotional pressure is relieved. A man who shares himself with someone else no longer feels alone.

It is important that you do not contradict his feelings. If you make judgments about his statements, he will clam up again. If he shares a strong feeling such as anger, you can respond, "Hey, sounds like you're a bit angry, perhaps even at me. That's OK. We all get angry. That doesn't mean we can't care about each other anyway. It's alright to be angry sometimes."

The mistake that so many lay counselors make is to jump in with advice or quick solutions. This is especially damaging when you are trying to help a depressed person. It shoves him right back down into despair and rejection. Instead of trying to solve his problem for him, try to gently draw him out. Ask sensitive questions, but avoid being pushy.

If the depressed person begins to open up, expect him to become angry. Remember that a major cause of depression is repressed anger. Listen in silence and accept his hostility. He will not be sinning if he expresses his anger, since no one will be hurt. Scripture tells us: "Be angry, and yet do not sin; do not let the sun go down on your anger" (Eph. 4:26). It is good for him to let out his anger.

We are commanded to help others who are weighed down and under stress. "Bear one another's burdens, and thus fulfill the law of Christ" (Gal. 6:2). Attentively listening to a depressed person is an excellent way to fulfill this ministry.

When the hostility comes, the depressed person will probably begin to feel guilty. In his own eyes he is merely proving that he is a terrible person. Often one who is suffering from depression will counter his negative, angry comments with positive ones, as if to undo what he has said about someone. It is important to reassure him about getting his feelings out in the open. Let him know that what he says to you will be kept in strict confidence, and make sure that this is so. Anything you can say or do to remove his guilt will enable him to fully express his hostility. This is the best thing for him.

When enough feelings come out, the depressed person often finds the source of his anger. When he gets down to the roots of his hostility, he is able to focus on the cause. The hostility is no longer "free-floating," so it cannot cause further long-term depression.

One of my clients was depressed for two weeks over a parking ticket. When he finally began to share his anger, I accepted it and encouraged him to go on. He got angry at the police department, and then he threatened to sue the city. We finally arrived at the root of his anger and depression: his father had forbidden him to drive as a teen-ager because he did not want his son to get a traffic ticket. This man's anger toward his father was not expressed during childhood, so it led to depression. Years later, with another person who listened supportively, he was able to share these feelings. However, if I had told him that a two-dollar parking ticket was nothing to get upset about, he might still be depressed.

Offer understanding and acceptance. When you listen to him, he begins to feel positively about you. He perceives that you are on his wavelength. Only if he believes that you understand and care will he begin to risk sharing his depression with you.

Imagine a little boy in tears who hops into the house on one leg. "Mom," he cries, "I scraped my knee on the sidewalk. It hurts!" Mom might look down and say, "You're not hurt! It's just a scratch, so go back out and play." A Band-aid may not even have been necessary, but now the wound only hurts more. The child needs understanding and care because the hurt and the fear are significant to him. Mom could have said, "Oh, you really hurt yourself! That stings, doesn't it? Let's put a Band-aid and a kiss on it." Now he feels secure. The pain and fear disappear, and he goes out to play as if it had never happened.

Unfortunately, many well-meaning Christians handle depression poorly. The depressed person does not need to hear any of the following:

"You just need to pray more often."

"Just have faith and you'll feel better."

"If you were in church more regularly, you'd be happier."

"Have you been reading your Bible enough?"

"Is there any unconfessed sin in your life?"

Although all of these things are important at the proper time, they certainly will not help the dejected soul who already feels he is not measuring up. Giving him more standards will only make him feel more guilty.

There are spiritual answers to give to the downhearted. It is unfortunate that Scripture verses implying guilt and worthlessness are often isolated by the depressed person, and more positive input is excluded. Make every effort to place Scripture in context. Use other verses to round out his misshapen view of God's relationship with man. He may be caught up in a concept that says, *I must die daily. I'm no good. Why should He die for me?* Share with him the unconditional, understanding love of God described in Matthew 6:25-29, John 3:16, Romans 5:8, and Romans 8:1,15-39. He needs to see that he is of value to

God, and that the Lord is not out to condemn him.

There is a difference between spiritual and emotional problems. A young woman shared her guilt feelings with two or three friends in her church and they responded "Well, just snap out of it! All you think about is yourself. If you would just get your mind off yourself, you wouldn't feel this way. Maybe the reason you're depressed is because God is convicting you of your self-centeredness."

This young lady was not self-centered by my standards. She was a perfectionist who was so guilt-ridden she could hardly cope with life. I doubt that her friends' comments did much to help her, spiritually or emotionally. Statements like these only encourage the depressed person to give up and withdraw. This kind of "counsel" may even be a step along the path that leads to suicide. Criticism and rejection are not the solution to depression; unconditional, accepting love is what this person needs.

Work out his problems together. When he has expressed his feelings and a trusting relationship has been established, show him new ways of coping with his feelings and behavior. Do this with words and by example. For instance, one of my clients had flunked out of dental school and he felt his whole world was crumbling. After we dealt with his feelings, we discussed other career opportunities that he might enjoy. I also shared what it was like to me to change vocations long after I was married and had children. Our conversation helped him to see that he had his whole life ahead of him, and he changed his attitude about it.

Often the depressed person has goals that are much too high for his own good. So it is important to help him set realistic goals. Bringing his aspirations down a peg or two will almost always relieve depression to the same degree.

Be consistently available. If depression is caused by a broken relationship, be a supportive stand-in to help ease the feelings of loss. A woman in my church called me with this kind of problem. She cried as she told me about a fight between herself and her daughter. Afterward the teen-ager had packed her bags and moved out in a fit of anger. Her mom understand-ably felt a great sense of loss. She talked it out with my wife and me, and she felt much better. When you lose someone you love, it always helps to know that others still care.

A final note of caution is in order. If depression comes and goes with no apparent cause; if it is chronic and inhibits the person's ability to cope with life; or especially if the depression is so deep that you are unable to help the victim and he or she seems suicidal, refer or take them to a qualified professional therapist as soon as possible.

However, much relief can be provided by the concerned lay counselor. Few things are more rewarding than sharing hope, support, and the light of love with those who walk in the shadow world of depression.

8

John the Baptist: Loner in the Wilderness

Our next biblical personality, John the Baptist, is very well known. John came at God's appointed time, he preached with power, and he did marvelous things to prepare for the Master's coming. He was a high achiever, and a servant of God to be admired. Jesus Himself said, "Truly, I say to you, among those born of women there has not arisen anyone greater than John the Baptist" (Matt. 11:11).

There are details in John's life, though, that show he was isolated; he separated himself from others. John's solitary nature points us to some of the characteristics of the extreme loner who is known as the schizoid personality type. The schizoid tends to break away from the world around him. John is like the loners of our society in that he was a man who spent his life in the wilderness; he was alone in the crowd.

JOHN IN THE BIBLE

Mark describes John's ministry as:

"THE VOICE OF ONE CRYING IN THE WILDERNESS,
'MAKE READY THE WAY OF THE LORD,
MAKE HIS PATHS STRAIGHT.'"

John the Baptist appeared in the wilderness preaching a
baptism of repentance for the forgiveness of sins. And all
the country of Judea was going out to him, and all the
people of Jerusalem; and they were being baptized by
him in the Jordan River, confessing their sins. And John
was clothed with camel's hair and wore a leather belt
around his waist, and his diet was locusts and wild
honey. And he was preaching, and saying, "After me
comes One who is mightier than I, and I am not even fit to
stoop down and untie the thong of His sandals. I baptized
you with water; but He will baptize you with the Holy
Spirit" (Mark 1:3-8).

John was the son of Zacharias, a priest of Israel. His mother,
Elizabeth, also came from a priestly line; she was in the line of
the daughters of Aaron. John was born about six months before
Jesus, so he was the forerunner prophesied in the Old Testa-
ment as the one who would come to tell the world that the
Messiah, the Lord Jesus Christ, was at hand.

The major part—perhaps thirty years—of John's life was
centered in the wilderness. Luke 1:80 tells us, "the child
continued to grow, and to become strong in spirit, and he lived
in the deserts until the day of his public appearance to Israel."
John wore desert clothes—camel's hair and a girdle of animal
skin. His diet was also taken from the desert—locusts and
wild honey. His life was that of a loner who came out of his
isolation to minister with a powerful message.

The *International Standard Bible Encyclopedia* notes that
John's desert habits have led some to connect him with the
Essenes, a monastic company of Jews. This commentary ex-
plains that there is little basis for the connection, other than
John's ascetic habits, and it states, "It was fitting that the one
who called men to repentance and the beginning of a self-

denying life should show renunciation and self-denial in his own life" (Grand Rapids: Eerdmans, 1949; vol. 3:1709).

THE TWENTIETH CENTURY WILDERNESS

Before describing the schizoid personality, the writer wishes to make clear that those who live alone or in a secluded environment are not necessarily extreme loners. Neither is it my contention that we are all schizoid personalities simply because at times we separate ourselves from the world around us. It is true, however, that we do tend to put distance between, or detach ourselves from others. For example, how many neighbors on your block do you know well?

The schizoid person, too, lives in the wilderness, though it is not necessarily made up of sun and sand. His desert is found in his own heart. In the counseling chamber, the schizoid personality shows two major characteristics.

He feels detached. He says, "It seems like I'm aware of everything that's happening around me, yet I always feel as though I'm really not part of the action." This is a typical statement therapists hear from the schizoid who is describing his lack of involvement with people.

One of my clients took a personality test, and it revealed that he was not involved with people. He found this hard to believe, for as he explained, "I'm with people all the time." It never occurred to him that he could be alongside others without being *with* people. If we do not let others affect us and if we do not invest in people, we are not really with anyone. If one does not have a sense of belonging, if he does not feel a warmth and acceptance coming from others, then his relationships with those around him are merely long distance.

The schizoid also often feels cut off and out of touch with his physical environment. It is as if he is asking, "Is the world real or not? Or is it just out of focus?" He easily loses his enthusiasm and his interest in life. He observes things at a distance without feelings and often experiences a sensation of depersonalization ("Am I really real?").

A client of mine named Mary is a good example of the loner personality. She lived in a small desert community in the Southwest and drove about two hundred miles each week to see me. She called me long distance on many occasions without having a definite purpose for her call. Mary had so little to talk about, yet she continued to call.

The schizoid person may display extreme anxiety. One client said, "When I get the feelings of being cut off I get very frightened and anxious, and I really don't know what to do." Another said, "Sometimes I don't want to be alone, but I can't stand crowds. They swallow me up. And if I accept your help I'll be subjugated to you. I'll lose my personality and be smothered."

Frequently the single adult who supposedly wants to marry complains: "When we start getting too close I feel like she's coming through too strong, and I lose my identity." Perhaps the problem is not that the other person is coming on too strong, but that the one who is troubled feels so weak that he or she perceives love and affection as something so strong that it threatens to smother them.

The schizoid person says, "I feel I love people in an impersonal way. I have no real emotions. I can't return tenderness. I can help people, but I can't enter into their joys and laughter." These are the statements of a lonely person.

THE HIGH PRICE OF WITHDRAWAL

The detachment and anxiety experienced by the schizoid person affect every part of his life.

He displays flat feelings and the inability to express emotions. How can a person be excited about a world from which he is withdrawing? I remember seeing a young man walking down a street in Los Angeles. He was looking straight ahead, not paying attention to anyone else, just singing to himself and lost in his own world. He was not concerned at the moment if anyone liked his singing nor did he care where he was going. He was oblivious to contact with people and the real world. This wandering singer is a graphic illustration of how the schizoid person lives.

At some time in his life, the schizoid felt pains that were beyond what he could handle. Somewhere in his past he decided that if he could shut off the feelings, the pain and the discomfort would go away. Therefore, his vital experiences of life are severely limited.

We experience life—the good and the bad, the joy and the sorrow—by feelings. Since the loner does not feel much, he cannot experience much pleasure. What he could not be expected to know is that when all the bad feelings are shut off, positive feelings are also stifled. Life without happy, warm feelings is a bleak existence. Better to be sad sometimes in order to feel joy and happiness later than to live alone inside oneself and feel nothing at all.

I hear countless vivid descriptions of what it is like to be alone in one's personal desert. One man told me, "Sometimes I feel just like a robot, like a mechanical man. I go through the motions, push the buttons, do things automatically—but I don't feel much of anything." A single man told me, "I meet an attractive girl and I want to marry her, but I'm incapable of falling in love." He really *could* fall in love; the problem is that love includes strong feelings of closeness. He is incapable of feeling, so he cannot experience the fullness of a deep, mature love.

Although the schizoid person expresses little emotion, he can be very angry inside without being aware of it. It is important that sooner or later a person begins to experience feelings—the positive and the negative. When one is aware of what he feels, he knows who he really is. If he never feels anything, then he will be permeated by a sense of depersonalization. He asks, "Who am I? Where am I going? Where do I fit in life?"

The schizoid is afraid that others will find out he is not a strong person. He thinks, *If you really get to know me you'll find out I'm weak.* Have you ever known someone who put on a tough, self-confident front but never let you close to him?

There is an interesting tale of two porcupines who were suffering through a cold night and decided to huddle together to avoid freezing. If they could just get close to each other, they would keep warm. The closer they got, though, the more they were stabbed by the other's quills. They had to lay close enough for warmth but not so close that they would get hurt. This is the way the schizoid personality lives, because he is afraid of being hurt. He wants to be close, but not too close. Love can be risky, but the schizoid exaggerates the risk. It is true that others may not always reciprocate when we reach out to them, but the mature person can handle occasional rejection and still be motivated to seek out and love others.

The schizoid is also petrified at the thought of dying. Some loners are obsessed by this fear. People are never truly ready to die until they know they have lived. If one has a weak ego and fears withdrawing into a never-never land, he may develop this excessive fear of dying.

He finds it difficult to form and maintain good "object relations." Objects in this sense are the people and things that are important to us. Relationships with objects, especially relationships with people, are necessary for our growth and emotional security. If a child loses its mother, a very significant object has been taken away. If your new car is demolished, here too you may feel depressed.

One of the things that thwarts good object relations is that the schizoid person subconsciously fears that his need for love is so great that he will demand too much and virtually devour the object of his love. He thinks, *I'm afraid I can't make moderate demands on people, so I won't make any demands at all.* A woman troubled by this fear dreamt that she was a giant vacuum cleaner, sucking hundreds of people into herself. The more people she collected, the more desperate she became; finally she dreamt she was drawing in all the people in the world.

The regrettable thing about the schizoid problem is that the loner has moved so far away from expressing his emotions in his relationships with people that there can be no growth. He is so starved for love that he is afraid love itself will be destructive. Love becomes dangerous. He thinks subconsciously, *If I make no demands, if I don't let myself feel like I need anybody, then I won't be hurt.* The dream about the vacuum cleaner reveals a schizoid who is afraid that in seeking love she will destroy the very people she needs.

While the depressed person fears losing someone or something he loves, the schizoid is fearful of the destruction of his ego. He is afraid he will cease to exist. The depressed person is worried about somebody loving him, but the loner is afraid of drawing so far into his own world that he will lose touch with the world around him.

Of course, we need to maintain a healthy balance in our interpersonal relationships. If I want you to be my friend, I need to be respectful and not demand unreasonable things from you. To borrow your lawn mower is one thing. To do it at 3 A.M., or keep it in my garage, is another. An invitation to dinner at a friend's house is fine, but dropping in with the wife and three young sons every evening at dinner time is not. Relatives who are visiting should apply the same principle. As a wise speaker once said, "Yes, go visit your family. Just remember, always pack a small suitcase." We can destroy relationships if we demand too much of them. However, the schizoid person has an unrealistic fear that any request will drive others away.

As a result, he tends to have many acquaintances, but no close friends. One client said, "I feel I want to get close to you, but I also want to be safe by staying separate. I feel like I want to stay in and go out, to read and not to read, to go to church and not to go. I have actually gone into a church, come right back out again, and then wanted to go back inside." These actions and feelings are symbolic of the schizoid's problem with people: he cannot stand to get too close. This ambivalence about being close explains why the schizoid person collects social acquaintances by the score but rarely develops a true friendship.

Consider Mary again, the woman who phoned me long distance. I noticed an interesting thing about her relationship with me. She related better on the telephone than in person. Why? It is another example of the "not-quite" adjustment. If she ever felt a swell of affection for me and I were only three feet away, it might terrify her. To be able to express feelings of warmth and love over the phone from two hundred miles away was safer. I am amazed at the amount of self-revelation a person shares over the telephone between sessions; they share things they would never tell me in the counseling chamber. Of course, this does not solve the real problem, which is the need to love and to relate deeply to another human being face to face. A telephone is a thing, not a person.

Another woman came to southern California one summer for therapy. Later that summer she said, "I like the way you conduct therapy and I want to continue with you, but I also want to go home to Washington. Can we have our session once a week on the phone?" Obviously this would not work. Even though it would be my voice and her voice doing the talking, there is something about being together—the human touch—that cannot be duplicated. I could answer questions by telephone, and she could find out if I was still there by telephone. Still, the human touch, the physical and emotional presence of someone who cares about you, is necessary.

He may have a high activity level. He always wants to go out and get involved. He says, for example, "I can hardly wait to get away from this house. It's so dull, I think I'll go to Palm Springs for the weekend." As soon as he gets to his destination he will ask, "Why in the world did I come out here? I think I'll go home." So the reservations are cancelled, but arriving home he says, "Now why did I come home? I think I should go back." On and on it goes, an endless back and forth existence.

Another young client said, "I decided to call mom and say I was coming over. She said that was fine, but when I hung up the phone I thought, *Now why did I call mom? I don't really want to go.* So I called her back and said I was too tired to come. She said that was all right; but when I hung up the phone, I felt I should have gone."

Rather than maintaining a high activity level, the schizoid may sometimes use boredom as a psychological defense. Those who have studied extensively in the field of human behavior know that boredom is a method of shutting out the world of feelings. When you are enjoying something, you cannot be bored. If a person feels nothing, there is nothing to enjoy, and boredom results.

Many feel the need to escape. They will run to the beach, the mountains, or the desert just to get away. Often they devote themselves solely to their work and live in a vivid fantasy life. Their daydreams, thoughts, and fantasies keep their minds occupied and provide a pseudolove that comes only from self.

You cannot say that this person is "on the outs" with people. Rather, he never quite gets *with it* with people. This has been called the "in and out program." I call it the not-quite relationship. The person is not quite with it, and he is not quite without it.

For instance, a woman told me, "I have two male friends I am really attracted to. I always want to be with one or the other, but I know this can't continue or I'll lose both of them. One of them kissed me and I enjoyed it. Now I feel like I have to run away from him. I'm in a constant furor of anxiety. I must see him—nothing else matters. But I don't go. I don't think I love him, but I need him desperately."

Do you hear the conflict, the feelings going on inside of her?

She is experiencing a self-made, not-quite relationship.

A bachelor of forty said, "If I kiss Ellen, my heart isn't in it. I hold my breath and count. I can only hug and love animals because they don't want anything from me." This helps us to understand why the schizoid personality is often a great animal lover. Of course, there is nothing wrong with having pets if you relate well with people, but some persons have been known to seclude themselves in a house, with the doors locked and the shades pulled down, and have surrounded themselves with dogs or cats for company.

DREAMS AND FANTASIES

A good analyst often examines his client's dreams as a key to understanding the person. Under the cloak of sleep we all deal with deep inner conflicts. Needs, wants, desires, and unexpressed feelings are resolved in the dream state, and without dreams none of us would stay sane for long. Like everyone else, the schizoid's conflicts are reflected in his dreams.

Here is a dream shared with me by a schizoid person: "I took off in a space ship, just floating about in empty space. At first I thought it was marvelous. There was nobody there to interfere with me. Then suddenly I panicked at the thought of not being able to get back."

This dream is an example of wish fulfillment. He wants to withdraw into a happy, perfect world, but something dreadful occurs to him when he does. His dream is to be understood in the light of a statement he made about himself: "Since I have no relationships with people and cut them off, I'm really alone." This also explains the anxious woman who calls me long distance just to find out if I'm there; she needs something to hold onto. The schizoid likes to withdraw; but as the dream suggests, that can be very frightening.

Here is another dream: "I was stranded on a tropical island, and there were lots of angry natives trying to get to me. I found a little hut on the shore. I rushed into it, locked the door and windows, and got into bed. Then I changed my mind and wanted to go out and enjoy the island, but I was afraid of the people. I had to stay alone, but that scared me too." Herein lies the whole story. This person had a weak ego and could not face the pressure of unfriendly people, so she stayed inside herself.

How to Help the Schizoid

We see schizoid manifestations every day in the people around us. One does not have to be severely disturbed to withdraw. All of us have said, "I don't know what's happening to him, but he appears to have gone into a shell." Or, "You know, it *seems* like Joe is listening to me, but I get the feeling he really only half listens to what I say. I feel like his mind is always somewhere else, like he's listening with one ear. He's always preoccupied." You may say of him, "He is very good at his job, but sometimes I wonder if he's human."

Often we find outgoing, enthusiastic, and efficient persons whose one mystery is that it is nearly impossible to know who they really are.

Withdrawal is often seen in those who believe that true spirituality involves separation from the world, from dealing with people, or from understanding and expressing our feelings. The model of our faith, though, must be the Savior. His love caused Him to reach down into the withdrawn, frightened state of man in sin and say, "I forgive you. I won't hurt you. Come and be mine. Tell me how you feel." Anytime our faith leads us away from solid, healthy relationships with people, it is wrongly applied.

Paul said, "I can do all things through Him who strengthens me" (Phil. 4:13). He is saying, in effect, "I go to the Lord in prayer; I seek Him out. Then I go back out and use the strength that I receive from solitude with Him. He helps me relate and be strong with people. But if I withdraw and just pray and meditate, I am only escaping from the world He wants me to reach." True love for Christ and faith in Him leads one to be more and more in touch with people for Him. Withdrawn, monastic pietists will not effectively reach a world that is hungering for Jesus.

The schizoid's therapeutic needs can be supplied by a patient, loving person who will do three things: listen, reflect, and model feelings. Most of all, the schizoid needs to gradually experience his feelings, to learn to trust and love others, and to find the true meaning of life in deep relationships with God and people.

Effective listening allows the schizoid to open up without fear of criticism or rejection. Much more will be said about listening in the final chapter, but it should also be mentioned here. The schizoid is a frightened, withdrawn person who is terrified of his own feelings and his need for love. He feels weak inside and is afraid to show his deepest emotions. Perfect love casts out fear, and the most loving thing you can do for him is to listen well. Allow the healing power of accepting silence to help him grow. He needs to experience feelings he may never remember feeling. Obviously he cannot deal with his feelings until he knows they exist, and supportive listening will help him discover himself.

In reflection the counselor states briefly how he thinks the person must feel. Discovery of feelings is possible when the counselor "plays back" the story to the withdrawn person. He tells what he was feeling as he heard the story or what he would have felt if he were in that person's shoes. For example, the counselor might say, "You know, if that guy had run into *my* wife's car, I think I would have been pretty upset for a while." Or, "It must be kind of sad and discouraging to lose the person you loved." You are reflecting the feelings he is sometimes afraid to look at.

In modeling feelings the counselor expresses maturely his own feelings. When he sees that you can laugh, cry, or even get angry, you will be modeling adult ways of experiencing feelings. Remember, a mature expression of how you feel is of utmost importance. Irresponsible gushing or uncontrolled anger are not mature emotional responses.

At this point the counselee begins to see and experience feelings through the person he is relating to, be it therapist or friend. At first he is frightened about feelings, especially the so-called negative emotions. Our society often brands anger and hostility as evil in themselves, even though everyone feels angry at times. When these feelings are experienced under healthy control, positive results can occur. It is normal to be angry, but we should not take it out on someone else unnecessarily. It is human to be sad. Jesus wept. It is not bad to be weak. "When I am weak," says Paul, "then I am strong" (2 Cor. 12:10). The withdrawn person will gradually face his emotions, both positive and negative, with the nonjudgmental support of one who shows that he cares about him.

It is obvious that what the schizoid person really needs is to be involved with people on a feeling level. Close personal relationships frighten him, so the counselor needs to help him deal with his fears. Again, the problem is that he fears he will lose his identity if anyone gets close to him. He needs to be told and shown gradually that to feel strongly about someone will not take away his identity.

You can communicate this vital message to him by sharing with him that you care and that you accept him. At the same time he will know that you are not demanding anything of him. Tell him he has the right to be who he is and to relate with you and that you will not expect anything from him that would threaten or frighten him away. Show him that you will share your feelings with him but will not force them upon him.

Schizoid persons are often paranoid. That is, they are frightened and suspicious of others. This results in part from the schizoid's tendency to project his feelings onto others. He sees the world as threatening and overpowering; and he assumes that what he feels, you feel as well. He needs to learn the difference between your acceptance of him and the feelings he assumes you have. When he states how he thinks you feel and act, gently tell him how you really feel. Point out the difference when there is one. He needs to learn to give others a chance to be who they really are, instead of what his fantasy imagines them to be.

The heart of the matter is his tendency to withdraw. Try to determine what painful experience he is withdrawing from. Work with him to change his life situation so that it no longer threatens him. Then help him to see that the problems he sees as overwhelming are not really that great.

When these steps are followed, the schizoid person will begin to experience feelings of warmth and a positive dependence. As he works through them and finds some genuine interpersonal love, his ego can develop and grow. This positive interaction with another human being is the best thing for him.

Step by step his growth through interaction with those who love him makes him decisive, positive, and aggressive in the healthy sense of the term. He is able to make decisions. He no longer withdraws; now he faces his problems. Instead of living in a fantasy world that does not fulfill his needs in the long run, he becomes emotionally involved with people. This makes life meaningful and much happier, for as God Himself said, "It is not good for the man to be alone" (Gen. 2:18).

9

Joseph,
the Healthy Person

Of all the people in the Bible, Joseph best represents healthy, well-balanced living. He is a powerful example of emotional maturity and mental health. His story is found in Genesis 37 through 50. A number of important things about his life and background help us to see why he was such a mature person.

LOVE MAKES ALL THE DIFFERENCE

It is clear that Joseph was loved as a child. "Now Israel loved Joseph more than all his sons, because he was the son of his old age; and he made him a varicolored tunic" (Gen. 37:3). Without any question, a person who is well-balanced emotionally must have received love and security in childhood. When a child does not receive enough love and attention, the results show up vividly in adolescent and adult life.

I enjoy being a therapist for this very reason. I am able to provide a second chance for my clients; they can work through some of the needs and feelings that were not resolved in childhood. Many persons need someone like an accepting, understanding parent to help them grow through their conflicts and areas of immaturity.

Some critics of Christian psychology imply that simply presenting the right Bible verse is always enough to change behavior and solve problems. However, Jesus is not merely interested in changed behavior. He cares about the heart. He wants men to be transformed, changed from within. Somewhere, somehow, the needs of the hurting must be met. Biblical therapy is one method the Holy Spirit can use to encourage the transformation of the heart.

Joseph was loved. In fact, Israel (formerly Jacob) favored his youngest son. Treating one child as special and more important than his siblings can spoil him, but this did not happen to Joseph. He demonstrated maturity by his ability to be away from home and accept responsibility without feeling sorry for himself. He was loved as a child, so he handled himself well in the face of trouble.

Joseph's brothers reacted quite differently. When one child gets all the love or the others feel that the parents are playing favorites, feelings flare up. Those who are deprived of affection are always the ones who rebel or become hostile. Joseph's brothers were no exception. To top it all, Joseph's dreams implied that one day his brothers would bow down to him. Although his brothers became angry, Joseph did not overreact to their feelings and actions. This is a clear sign of maturity.

OBEDIENCE MATTERS

When Joseph's brothers were in the fields with the flocks and herds, Jacob told him to find out how they were doing. Apparently Jacob did not know how much his other sons hated their younger brother. Joseph must have known, but he followed instructions without question.

Jacob said: "Go now and see about the welfare of your brothers and the welfare of the flock; and bring word back to me" (Gen. 37:14). Imagine how Scripture might read if Joseph had responded to authority as many persons do today:

> Are you kidding? Those guys are out to get me. Besides, it's hot out there and I don't appreciate hiking through the desert, so don't tell me what to do.

Or, if he had made a promise that was never kept:

> OK, dad, just as soon as I get time.

One sign of neurosis is the inability to take orders and follow instructions. This problem is typical of Esau's type, the impulsive person. The well-balanced person like Joseph can follow orders without argument or complaint.

Joseph not only heard his father, he also went into action. Obedience is not just verbal agreement; we must also carry out instructions. Joseph went to the fields. He knew the value of obedience to proper authority. Obedience is a virtue. Granted it is not always easy, but cooperating with leaders whenever possible is a sign of mental health.

HANGING IN THERE

Bad things happen even to those who are upright. Misfortune is a part of life on this planet, and so it was with Joseph. When he got to the fields, his brothers attacked him, tore off the cloak his father had given him, and threw him into a pit. He had had better days, to say the least!

Joseph's brothers even plotted to kill him, though one of them came up with a better idea. "We don't like him, but we don't have to kill him. We can sell him and make a little profit for ourselves." Note that those who are emotionally imbalanced often do not care who they hurt. Although his brother Reuben wanted him kept safe, Joseph was sold to a trader's caravan for twenty pieces of silver and taken to Egypt. His brothers tore his coat, dipped it in animal blood, and showed it to their father. Jacob believed that his youngest son had fallen prey to wild animals. He mourned and could not be comforted, believing he would never see his son again.

What about Joseph? How would he handle the stress of a new life? If you catch an uptight, paranoid person off guard, he cannot adjust. The obsessive type who has to have everything structured and logical, would be upset with the change in circumstances. It is difficult to get him to have fun or laugh at a party, much less to redo his life. A strong characteristic we see in Joseph's life was his ability to cope with a new situation. He did not need routine in order to be secure.

How would you feel in Joseph's place? What would you do? Separated from home and family. Reduced from favorite son to common slave. Sold to a stranger in a foreign land. Alone. Tired. Deprived of everything familiar and homelike. How would you cope?

The Bible does not tell us that Joseph was depressed and gave up. Because he had a strong self-concept, he found in himself the ability to face life, even disappointment, and not allow circumstances to destroy him. He did the best he could with what he had. As we shall see, he surprised everyone and made his dreams come true.

JOSEPH PROSPERS

Joseph found himself serving in the house of Potiphar, the captain of Pharaoh's bodyguard. As Scripture says, "And the LORD was with Joseph, so he became a successful man" (Gen. 39:2). Another aspect of emotional health is productivity. Joseph was capable of producing something worthwhile, of setting goals and reaching them.

Sometimes an emotionally unstable person is so busy compensating for his compulsions, depression, or anxiety that he has no emotional energy left for work and creativity. This problem is not unlike that of having an automobile with a large chassis and a very small engine. You cannot drive anywhere because it takes all the power the engine can muster to move the car in and out of the garage. There is not enough power left to get under way. In the same sense, most emotionally distraught persons are not fully productive because their emotional energy is tied up in defending themselves.

When a person feels emotionally secure, he can study better or work longer hours with less fatigue. A neurotic person usually sleeps poorly and wakes up tired. Then he is keyed up at night and afraid to go to bed. But as his ego grows and he approaches emotional maturity, he feels more rested, more excited about life, more able to cope. This was true of Joseph, who became overseer in his master's house because of his ability to produce.

No!

Apparently Joseph was also a good-looking man. Potiphar's wife became enamored of him and turned on the charm. She tried to seduce Joseph, approaching him directly. "And it came about after these events that his master's wife looked with desire at Joseph, and she said, 'Lie with me'" (Gen. 39:7).

Imagine the stress this put on Joseph. He was a single young man with the same intense sexual needs as anyone else. Yet he had been put in charge of his master's household, and he was loyal to Potiphar. He found himself torn between personal values of loyalty and chastity and the seductiveness of an attractive woman. But Joseph was mature. He had the ability to say no.

A neurotic person, who needs everyone's approval, finds it nearly impossible to say no. He accepts every invitation, rather than to risk offending anyone. He may take on more work and responsibility than he can handle, just to avoid refusing a request. A sign of positive self-image and emotional balance is the ability to say no when it is appropriate. It is not necessary to please everyone. In fact, it is impossible to do so.

The incident with Potiphar's wife shows another side of Joseph's maturity. His response was kind but very firm. His refusal to succomb to her invitation demonstrates clearly that he was not given to immediate gratification. Joseph could say no to himself as well as to others.

WHEN BAD TURNS TO WORSE

Being a psychologist has risks. For instance, a client may become so upset that he tries to hurt the therapist or his family. One client found out my address and came to the door one evening. My wife was home alone, and he came in uninvited. His first question was, "If Dr. Sall dies, will you marry me?" He also wanted to know how much life insurance I had. I arrived home just a few minutes later, in time to avert what might have been a tragedy. My wife handled the situation well, but it was a scary night!

A similar incident involved a woman I had been counseling as a young pastor. I recognized her efforts to seduce me and referred her immediately to a female therapist. However, if the sexual advances of a neurotic person are rejected, the result is extreme hostility. I later learned that the woman reacted in blind fury. She threatened to call the elders of my church and accuse me of trying to seduce her. In her anger, she was ready to destroy me and my ministry.

This is exactly what Potiphar's wife did to Joseph. He did the right thing, but in her anger she tried to destroy him. She lied to her husband, telling him that Joseph had tried to make love to her. Potiphar's anger blazed, and he had Joseph thrown into jail. Joseph was faithful to his master, but his reward was the dungeon.

It is one thing to rob a bank and end up in jail. One might say that the robber got what was coming to him. But if you see a burning house, rush in to save three children at the risk of your own life, and then are accused of setting the fire—how does that feel? This must have been the disappointment Joseph felt.

Joseph's maturity came through again. He was able to roll with the punches. He could take life in stride and not let adversity destroy him. If a man is thrown in jail unjustly, he can do one of two things. He can moan and blame God, allowing the bitterness to eat away at him. Or he can face the situation realistically and say, "Well, I don't belong in jail, so I'll get my lawyer and family to work on it from the outside. Meanwhile, I now have a chance to catch up on my reading. Maybe this is the Lord's way of giving me a little rest. Besides, it's nice not to have the phone ringing all the time."

Joseph did not succumb to bitterness. This does not mean that he was not angry at what happened to him. He probably was angry, but he did not let his anger control him and ruin his life. He channeled his anger constructively instead of taking it out on others. Later in his life we find him putting his brothers to the test, but not with the intent of revenge or destruction. His purpose was their growth.

How much can one man take? How long can a mature faith last? Ask Joseph. He never gave up. He did not become bitter and hateful. He did not blame God for the actions of men. No matter how bad things got, he was able to support and help others.

Joseph was soon placed in charge of all the prisoners in the jail. Pharaoh's cupbearer and baker were there due to the ruler's displeasure with them. Joseph interpreted their dreams and asked them to mention his name to Pharaoh when they were released from jail. The baker was hanged, but the cupbearer was restored to his position. He promptly forgot all about Joseph.

Often people will ask for help and then forget about you when you need them. It is easy to be taken advantage of. It is rare that we are appreciated. The cupbearer got what he wanted, but he did not care about the young man who helped him. Still, Joseph was patient. He waited. He continued to be productive. He trusted God, and his time came.

IF MY FRIENDS COULD SEE ME NOW!

Two years later, Pharaoh had a dream. The cupbearer finally remembered Joseph, and he was brought from prison to interpret the dream. He explained the upcoming seven years of plenty and seven years of famine. Pharaoh was so impressed with Joseph that he named him second in command of the Egyptian empire. Joseph organized the nation to save Egypt from starvation. The grain was stockpiled and when the famine struck, only Egypt had food. All the neighboring peoples came to Egypt to buy food from Joseph. Thus the famine opened the door for Joseph's long-awaited encounter with his brothers. They came to buy grain from him, not realizing that the ruler before whom they bowed was the brother they had sold into slavery.

Joseph had a mature love for his brothers. He was concerned with their growth, so he devised a test for them. Because they did not recognize him, he was able to demonstrate graphically the wrong they had done. His brothers reacted responsibly because of the lesson they learned through Joseph. His purpose was not to get revenge but to discipline. Hate punishes, but love teaches.

THE FREEDOM TO FEEL

In 1962, our nation's attention was focused on the first orbital space flight. Now, in the days of moon exploration, it seems like such a simple maneuver to orbit the earth. At the time, though, it was a magnificent feat. The thing that struck me most about the event was the human touch of the family reunion after touch-down.

The astronaut, a man of tremendous courage, had just shown his great skills by being the first person to orbit the earth alone. In the aftermath his personal strength was evident in his ability to show his emotions openly. His family was there as he ran into his wife's arms. He was not afraid to show the world that he loved his family and that it was good to be back safe. A mature person is able to show affection, to weep, to have a good belly laugh, and to share his feelings.

I want my staff to feel free to interact with me; so for this reason my wife and I hosted a staff Christmas party. Twenty people came to our home for dinner, and of course we had a "white elephant" gift exchange. There were several fine gifts, like coasters, aftershave, and pen sets. My gift was a piece of toilet bowl, two bent cuff links, and an old automobile thermostat, all placed in a used cigar box. I got the neck of the chicken, so to speak.

In any case, it was encouraging to watch several men with doctoral degrees in psychology let down their hair and have a good time. When they clown around, it is exciting to be with them. They are emotionally strong and healthy because they are not afraid to feel, to have a good time and even to cry.

The same was true of Joseph. He wept at the sight of his brothers standing before him in Egypt. He had to leave the room at one point to avoid giving away his identity. He loved them, missed them, and was glad to see them. He also longed to see his father and the brother from whom he had been separated so long, as a result of his older brothers selling him into slavery.

Joseph is a perfect picture of a man who was able to become genuinely involved with other people. Although he had been hurt, he was able to overcome this and love his brothers anyway. He had developed the capacity for good object relations. He did not need to act out in anger as Esau did. He was not like the schizoid personality, who withdraws from people. He did not hold grudges or demand rigid obedience to rules as did the Pharisees. Because of his ability to relate well to others, Joseph forgave his brothers. He wept with them and took care of them. He shared everything he had and was with them. He knew how to love.

"I AM JOSEPH"

This brilliant young ruler of Egypt had a healthy identity. He identified himself to his brothers by saying, "I am Joseph." So his self-image was based on his personhood, not on his works or external identity. He could have said, "I am the Most High Potentate, Ruler of all Egypt, Master of the Nile, Second only to Pharaoh." But all he said was, "I am Joseph." He did not try to impress everyone with his beautiful wife, well-bred children, and split-level palace on the hill with a two-chariot garage. He was in touch with himself. He had a realistic estimate of his inner identity.

The Bible says that Joseph's brothers were troubled at his presence. "Terrified" is a good way to say it. His first question to them after revealing his identity was, "Is my father still alive?" He was more concerned with love and family ties than with revenge. Imagine, though, the anxiety that the brothers must have felt. What would he do with them? Those who had wanted to kill him were now in his hands. Besides, he ruled the only nation that had food, and their land was starving. In their minds, Joseph was power personified.

"Then Joseph said to his brothers, 'Please come closer to me.' And they came closer. And he said, 'I am your brother Joseph, whom you sold into Egypt'" (Gen. 45:4). So Joseph spoke firmly and to the point. He did not avoid issues nor mince words. He told the truth.

Some Christians hold that we should never confront others. However, it is one thing to turn the other cheek, but it is quite another to avoid issues and confrontation. Other Christians believe that we should not speak up in the face of adversity. It is as if God's own people should be mushy rather than display intestinal fortitude. But this is not so, and Joseph is an example of a person who dealt with the hard truth.

When he identified himself as "the one you sold into slavery," he was asserting himself at the proper time and with the proper motive. He made his brothers accountable for their actions. They learned through Joseph's loving discipline what they would not have learned through harsh judgment.

THE LIVING KEY

One of the by-products of a healthy personality is increased faith. A healthy person is one who faces life openly, who recognizes his limitations and trusts God implicitly to work everything out.

Faith does not thrive within a legalistic system. If a child hears only do's and don'ts, should's and ought's from his parents, he will likely grow up concentrating on the rules of Christianity rather than on his relationship with God and his fellow man. He will view God purely as an authority figure. All he will know of religion is right and wrong, black and white, good and evil. He will never be able to enjoy a knowledge of the grace of God, because he views God as Judge rather than as a loving Father.

Faith does not rebel against responsibility to authority. If the child receives inconsistent discipline and guidance, or no discipline at all, he will learn to mistrust authority. He will grow up rebelling against God as an authority figure. Rather than trust God, the rebellious person spends his whole life trying to prove he needs no one, least of all his Creator.

Joseph was blessed with the wondrous discovery that saved him from both legalism and rebellion. His life was guided by true faith. Joseph trusted God, even when things looked darkest. The fully victorious Christian life belongs to the healthy personality who is still able to believe that faith in the living God is important and valuable and meaningful. Joseph recognized who God is and then trusted Him to work everything out in His own time.

After Jacob died, his sons feared that Joseph would have them killed. "When Joseph's brothers saw that their father was dead, they said, 'What if Joseph should bear a grudge against us and pay us back in full for all the wrong which we did to him!'" (Gen. 50:15). Joseph's mature response was to forgive: "But Joseph said to them, 'Do not be afraid, for am I in God's place? And as for you, you meant evil against me, but God meant it for good in order to bring about this present result, to preserve many people alive'" (Gen. 50:19-20).

Joseph's ability to love and care for others was directly related to his undying faith. He could forgive his brothers because of his personal relationship with God. He said, in effect, "You meant to do me in, and sold me into slavery. It was not always easy for me in Egypt. I missed you all, and my father. Even when I did a good job in Potiphar's household, I was thrown into jail unjustly. I helped the cupbearer, and he forgot all about me. I spent two more years in prison. But I didn't give up. I was secure in my God, and He prospered me. I was put in charge of other prisoners. Life got a little easier in the jail. Finally I was taken before Pharaoh to interpret his dream.

"Now I am a ruler. Though you wanted to kill me, my brothers, I saw beyond all the circumstances to the God of our fathers. He used the evil of what happened to me to provide food for His people. I trusted Him, knowing amidst the unfairness that God had a purpose. That's why I'm here today and that's why I forgive you. God was in control all the time, so I have no need for grudges or bitterness."

Only a man with a healthy personality could make such a statement. Only a soul possessed of deep, honest faith could live such a life without bitterness. God does keep books, and Joseph knew it. He waited on the Lord to make things right. In spite of the ups and downs of life, Joseph grew into a wise and loving person. He achieved a strong faith and a strong life by recognizing who God is and "selling out" to Him. By trusting God, Joseph was able to love, to forgive, to produce, to hope, and to rejoice as few men have. Faith as God intended it is the key to abundant life.

10

The Counselor
Within You

As I travel from place to place as a public speaker, many persons tell me they identify with and recognize the various personality types discussed here. They also ask what they can do to help others grow toward emotional maturity. Each of the preceding personality studies concludes with a section on therapeutic needs, but I would be remiss to close this volume without sharing further on this matter. There are some basic, but quite effective, techniques that can be used in counseling others who come to you for help.

By way of brief summation, it can be said that all people who have personality problems do one of three things to a harmful extreme. They are either moving toward people, moving away from people, or moving against people. Those who move toward others often have deep clinging-vine dependency needs and often live in a state of depression. The persons who move away from others are, of course, obsessive and schizoid personalities; they avoid emotional involvement with people.

They shut off all feeling and communication and work things out independently in words and actions or by means of an internal fantasy world. The third category, moving against people, includes Esau and other character disorder types. The person with an extreme character disorder both expresses attitudes and does things that damage others.

It is true that what might help one person would only harm another. There are times in the therapeutic process when one method helps a particular client, and another should be saved until later. The techniques to be listed here, though, are basic to establishing a good supportive relationship in counseling. If the following steps are applied as you relate with persons who hurt, then you will have laid a good foundation for their growth and eventual happiness.

QUIET: GROWTH IN PROGRESS

The greatest difference between a professional counselor and an amateur is this: the amateur counselor talks too much. He thinks he must have an answer to every problem. He feels he must give helpful advice. What he does not know is that his compulsion to talk actually gets in the way of the other person.

Imagine someone who is telling you about a personal problem. He is just beginning to become emotionally involved in it and is opening up to you. The common reaction from the listener is to cut him off and say, "I know just what you mean! I've been through exactly the same thing!" And then he is off like a whirlwind, discussing his own problem. The person who was beginning to reach out and share immediately thinks, *He doesn't even care enough about me to really hear me out.* Counseling technique number one, then, and probably the most effective means of helping people, is to be silent.

When I first started my career as a therapist, I used to feel a bit guilty. I said to myself, "These people are paying me money to help them, and all I'm doing is listening." Yet I know that it works. Many people have listened to someone talk out a problem; when the conversation was over, the other person will say, "You know, you just don't realize how much you've helped me." After he is gone, all you can do is throw your hands in the air and exclaim, "Help? All I did was listen!" Simple as it seems, listening is why you were able to help him.

Let us take a close look at the technique of silent listening. What does it do for the person who needs someone? What does it say to the person who comes for help? It says first of all, "I accept you." A depressed person, for example, is loaded with guilt and anxiety, and he feels that he is worthless. If you listen, he feels free to talk out his feelings, his views, his fears. If he feels guilty and expects you to judge him and criticize him, your silence says something entirely different to him. Patient, accepting silence says, "It's all right for you to have an opinion. It's all right for you to feel that way. It's all right for you to think that way." In the past he felt that everything he did was wrong, and he was constantly criticized. As you listen, he learns that his past experiences and feelings about them are not appropriate for today. Now, someone is willing to hear him out and accept him.

Another reason silence is so effective is that it allows the real problem to emerge. Often clients will come to me for the first session of therapy and talk endlessly about trivial matters, just to avoid facing the real problem. Sometimes they do not even know what the problem is; all they know is that they are unhappy or not coping well. Silence does the trick because it allows the surface layers of defensiveness, denial and fear to slowly melt away. This brings the real difficulty to the fore and enables the counselor to help.

Often the person's real difficulties do not surface until after several counseling sessions in which the counselor has listened carefully and gained the trust of the counselee. Only then will the hurting person feel free to talk about the problem. The obsessive person may talk a great deal about his problems, but there is no feeling, no emotional tone, when he talks.

Sometimes one must remain silent until the counselee has run out of things to talk about. Then his real feelings will emerge because your silence has built trust.

Emotional problems and interpersonal difficulties always bring with them a measure of bottled-up pressure and tension. Silence is one of the best ways to help relieve this pressure. The counselee says, "Oh, it feels so good just to be able to talk this out. It's nice to talk where nobody stops me, where I can just let it go, and not worry about what I'm saying or why." Even people with severe emotional problems have felt tremendous relief after only one or two sessions with a psychologist. They feel nearly cured (though they are not!) just because the pressure is relieved.

A fourth reason why silence is so effective is that it allows the person to work toward his own solution. Giving advice is *not* the best thing to do in most cases. The chronically dependent, passive person does not need answers from us. He needs to think it through, to use his own faculties, his own reasoning and judgment. He needs to find his own solution. If we supply ready-made answers, the dependent person will always need us. We will be helping him the most if we allow him to talk it out and come to his own conclusion. Similarly, the rebellious person with a character disorder would probably not even listen to our advice, in fact, he might do just the opposite. It is better to listen supportively and let the person work out a solution that satisfies him best. Silence, then, is perhaps the greatest tool we have in helping another person.

THE CLARIFYING QUESTION

As good as it is, silence cannot solve all problems. Some people will ramble on for hours and never get to the point. Some may be unable to discover what is wrong. Neither will the counselor be able to help in this case unless he asks an appropriate, insightful question. A question is often effective in directing the person toward the central problem.

If a person comes to me and talks for a half hour about the football game he saw on television last week, I may ask the question, "I'm sure you enjoyed the football game, but I really don't think that is why you came to see me. I'm wondering, what is your problem?" And sometimes in the course of conversation a client will get too close to something that bothers him, and he will veer off in another direction. The question then might be: "I notice that you were talking freely before, then your face flushed and you quickly changed the subject. I'm wondering if there was something there you didn't want to face."

Questions can be very important in helping a person focus on himself and his problems. A note of caution is in order, though. A depressed person or the obsessive with an overactive conscience can be harmed by too many questions being asked. It is wise to avoid asking too many questions because the overly guilty, burdened person takes questions as criticism. It is as though he were being needled by a parent: "Why did you do that? Why did you say that? Why aren't you doing it this way?" Questions can easily be interpreted as being judgmental.

Questions should be used appropriately. For example, questions directed toward the obsessive person only prime his verbal pump and cause him to talk even more. What he needs is lots of silence. This allows him to run out of things to say, and then his feelings will finally begin to surface. On the other hand, a person in deep depression finds it very difficult to talk. He broods and withdraws as much as he can. Gentle questions help him to begin communicating with you. If a person seeking help is frightened, he may need a bit of questioning on subjects other than the problem area. This will help him to feel safe so that he can talk about the problem freely. Many times I have asked a counselee, "How many brothers or sisters do you have? What part of the country did you come from?" These questions are simple, but they help to get the person used to the idea of talking and using his voice. Once the person begins to talk freely, it is wise to dispense with questioning and employ as much silence as possible.

On the other side of the spectrum, questions are extremely useful in dealing with the impulsive person. He tends to act now and think later. What he needs is to develop some structure in his personality so that he does not act things out on the primitive level of impulses. Questions help create self-evaluation. Questions about his future and his goals help him to move away from himself, observe his own behavior, and make some long-range plans for improvement.

Questions are also helpful in clearing up confusion. If you cannot understand what the other person is saying, or if his statements make no sense, properly timed questions put things in better focus. Often the gushy, hysterical personality will contradict himself in the process of talking about his problems. When little or no mature thinking exists, the counselee may not be in control of his statements. One might point out to him, "Ten minutes ago you told me you hated your mother. Now you are telling me you love your mother. Which is it? Or do you hate her for some things and love her for others?" Questions can help, then, to tighten up a person's statements about his feelings; and, as a result, his personality will become more structured.

"Stop and Look at Yourself!"

Next on our list of counseling techniques is confrontation. This method is absolutely essential in dealing with the person with a character disorder, like Esau. A common statement of confrontation I might make in therapy would be, "Hey, take a look at what you are doing. Take a good look at what you are doing."

One day a young man got very angry in my office; he picked up a lamp and smashed it to bits. I immediately asked him to look at what he had done. He was so angry at his father that he had lost his sense of where he was and what he was doing. He needed to be confronted, so I said, "John, you are in my office. You're not at home. And I'm not your father. Look what you're doing. You're destroying someone else's property." Confronting him in this way provided the external control that momentarily compensated for the internal control he lacked.

People with a defective conscience and few internal controls often need therapy that includes confrontation. Another statement that I commonly use is, "Consider what you just said." A married woman once said in my office, "I'm so mad at my husband I'm going home to kill him. We've got a gun at home. It's in my bedroom vanity. I can find it, . . . and we've got plenty of shells. As soon as I leave here, I'm going to kill him." In her feelings of anger and vengefulness, she was losing touch with reality and her responsibility. She was nearly overcome by her hostile feelings.

I said to her quite loudly, "Did you hear what you just said? You said that when you left here you are going to go home and kill your husband. Do you realize what you said? Are you really going to do that?"

She replied, "Well, I really didn't mean that I was going to kill him. I just mean that I'm terribly angry at him."

I responded, "You must learn to talk about your feelings more. You cannot act them out without causing damage to yourself or someone else."

Here is a statement I use in dealing with angry people who are holding a grudge: "Maybe your anger is hurting you more than him. You'd like to get even with him; but after all this time has gone by, you are still the angry one. You are not getting even with him; he's actually continuing to punish you. You're hurting yourself more by hanging on to your anger and bitterness."

What about the young man who has been doing a lot of sexual acting out? I say, "I think you're sleeping with all these women to prove you're really a man. You don't really feel like a man inside." I point out to him that his real problem is one of masculinity, not of conquests or accomplishments.

How about the victim of chronic self-induced migraine headaches? I tell this person, "Every time you withdraw into a shell, you're only making your headaches worse. Do you want to go through life torturing yourself? Why don't you face the fact that your problems won't disappear if you withdraw? By facing your troubles, you'll conquer them. Then you won't have to suffer from these terrible headaches."

Sometimes even a very brief statement can do wonders. For example, we might say, "I feel you're avoiding something" or "You're behaving destructively." Confrontation directs the person to look objectively at who he is and what he is doing. Confrontation makes him aware of what he is doing to himself with his behavior.

FINDING THE MYSTERY MEANING

A knowledgeable layman who has a heart for ministering to others can do wonders in personal counseling. I trust that this volume will help you to reach a larger number of people and to understand various types of personalities. It is my personal conviction that sensitive laymen can be good counselors by listening in silence, by asking gentle, clarifying questions, and by having the strength to confront those who need it. However, I believe that the fourth primary technique of counseling separates the professional from the nonprofessional counselor. This is what is known as interpretation.

A qualified therapist uses the first three techniques to help him detect when a feeling or memory is about to be uncovered from the person's sub-conscious mind. Many symptoms and behaviors are rooted in the subconscious, and the resolution of conflict often requires conscious awareness of the problem. A skilled therapist assists in this movement toward conscious awareness by interpreting the real meaning behind statements, dreams, and fantasies. Because of the complex and volatile nature of subconscious mechanisms, however, I do not recommend that untrained persons attempt to make interpretations.

We can provide first aid at the scene of an accident if we know some basic lifesaving techniques. We can also nurse a person back to health by spending time with him and supplying his medical needs. However, it would be foolish for us to attempt brain surgery without extensive medical training. In the same way, you can be quite effective in counseling others, but interpretation is a technique to be used only by professional counselors. Much damage can be done by the well-meaning person who lacks the proper skills. This does not in any way diminish the significant growth that can result from listening, questioning, and confronting. However, some things in the therapeutic process should be left to professionals who have adequate training.

For the sake of clarification let us examine the case of a young mother who had fantasies in which she killed her children. She was shocked and afraid because she also loved her children. On a simple interpretive level, one might say that she was displacing onto the children hostility that she felt toward her husband, employers, or parents. According to this interpretation, she needed to rid herself of hostile feelings. She picked the children because they were the easiest target and because they could not retaliate. On a deeper level of interpretation, however, the true problem came to light.

When she was a little girl, this woman had always sought the approval of her father. But try as she might, she never felt she had his attention and support. She knew that he had always wanted a son, but this son was never born. She felt that her father's cold, rejecting manner was due to the fact that she was not a boy. Although she could not have understood this as a little girl, the need for her father's love caused her to think, *If only I could become a boy, then daddy would love me. Then daddy would accept me.*

Rejection in her childhood caused her to hate her own children. Why? Children reminded her that she was a woman and that she had brought them into the world. Secondly, she remained at home to care for the children while her husband was in the business world. This further isolated her from the role of a male. The problem could not be solved until she became aware of this deep desire to be accepted by her father.

With proper counseling over a period of time and a few gentle, but very accurate, interpretations, she gradually became aware of her need for her father's approval. In the care of a male counselor, she transferred her needs and feelings and worked through the problem satisfactorily. She is now an emotionally full-grown woman who loves her children without reservation. She has no need to harm them. She no longer needs to be a male. The key to her improvement was the accurate interpretation of her deep subconscious problem.

Interpretations vary according to the depth of the emotions involved. If a cat walks into the room, someone might say, "Boy, that cat sure looks angry today." We would say that this person is projecting his hostility onto something else, rather than deal with it himself. When a counselee talks factually about someone he claims to be close to, we would interpret this as a lack of feeling. If he reports no feelings about the experience or the person he is describing, we know he is defending against something.

Another area of interpretation, of course, is the content and meaning of dreams. Man dreams in symbols. His dreams condense all past and present wishes and desires, as well as the day's "leftover" feelings and conflicts, into one composite subconscious experience. Dream interpretation is therefore quite complex and requires skill and training.

A Closing Pep Talk

The best counselor is the one who is most in touch with himself. One cannot expect to help others if he is hiding from himself. Have you identified with any of the Bible characters presented in this volume? Did you see any of their fears or behavior in yourself? Perhaps you have discovered new areas of growth and maturity that the Lord wishes you to appropriate. Perhaps, on the other hand, you are already beginning to deny those things you discovered about yourself in these pages.

Let me encourage you to do as the Scriptures say: "You shall love the Lord your God with all your heart, and with all your soul, and with all your strength, and with all your mind; and your neighbor as yourself" (Luke 10:27). Love God. Be open with Him. Be honest with Him. Let Him teach you, guide you, bless you. Be open to His love, and do not put Him in a box labeled "Religion." God is a triune Personality. Let Him counsel you.

Also, love others as you do yourself. If you are down on yourself, you will be down on others or at least too depressed to help them.

If you drive yourself into a life of endless performance, you will expect too much of others as well. You will never know them or your own real feelings.

If you exercise no control over what you say and do, you will drive others away. Develop maturity and self-control, and you will gain the love and respect of others.

If you withdraw and hide from yourself and your emotions, you will also withdraw from meaningful relationships with others. Life is not meant to be lived alone.

Be in touch with God. Be in touch with yourself. Be in touch with others. That is the purpose of this book. May it be the purpose of your life.